Roger Lamb's American Revolution

ALSO BY DON N. HAGIST

These Distinguished Corps:
British Grenadier and Light Infanty Battalions
in the American Revolution

Noble Volunteers:
The British Soldiers Who Fought the American Revolution

The Revolution's Last Men:
The Soldiers Behind the Photographs

British Soldiers, American War:
Voices of the American Revolution

Wives, Slaves, and Servant Girls:
Advertisements for Female Runaways in America, 1770–1783

ROGER LAMB'S AMERICAN REVOLUTION

A British Soldier's Story

A NEW EDITION

Edited by DON N. HAGIST

WESTHOLME
Yardley

Westholme Publishing, LLC
904 Edgewood Road
Yardley, Pennsylvania 19067
Visit our Web site at www.westholmepublishing.com

ISBN: 978-1-59416-397-5
Also available as an eBook.

Printed in the United States of America.

This is a soldier's story.
When thinking of soldiers, think not of
allies and enemies, of good and bad,
but of individuals, each with a story.

CONTENTS

LIST OF ILLUSTRATIONS VIII
INTRODUCTION IX

1. *Early Life in Dublin* 1
2. *Service as a Soldier in Ireland* 7
3. *Voyage to America* 17
4. *Campaign in Canada, 1776* 31
5. *Burgoyne's Expedition* 40
6. *Imprisoned with the Convention Army* 67
7. *First Escape to New York* 75
8. *Southern Campaign, 1780* 86
9. *Campaign and Surrender, 1781* 98
10. *Second Escape to New York* 119
11. *Return to Great Britain* 148

APPENDIX: JOURNAL OF THREE SERJEANTS OF THE 23RD REGIMENT 175
SOURCES 179
RECOMMENDED READING 181
INDEX 183

ILLUSTRATIONS

Roger Lamb's enlistment in the 9th Regiment of Foot 9

Private soldier of the 9th Regiment of Foot, 1775 13

Lamb and Sergeant Clarke in the Black Hole 23

The 9th Regiment firing on American Boats 47

Corporal of the 9th Regiment, 1777 59

Barracks for Prisoners outside Boston, 1777-1778 69

R. Lamb made to run the Gauntlet 71

Roger Lamb's enlistment into the 23rd Regiment 85

Sergeant of the 23rd Regiment of Foot, 1779 91

Crossing the Catawba River, 1781 103

Battle of Guilford Courthouse, 1781 113

Lamb's captivity in Frederick Town 125

Encampment of the Convention Army at Charlotte Ville 131

Sergeant Lamb and his party persuading the deserter 137

The American Friend bringing us Provisions 143

Example of a soldier's discharge 151

Roger Lamb's pension examining board record 153

Roger Lamb 171

INTRODUCTION

Of all the British soldiers who served in North America during the American Revolution, none wrote more than Roger Lamb. The Dublin native spent only twelve years in the army—much shorter than the twenty, thirty or more years of many of his fellow soldiers. Unlike all but a few, he wrote of his experiences, and wrote of them more extensively than any other. He certainly had a lot to say—his service on two major campaigns put him in the thick of some of the war's most famous battles. Moreover, he was twice captured and twice escaped, making his way through hostile territory to rejoin the British army. Later in his life he wrote two books chronicling these experiences in great detail. Hundreds of British soldiers went through similar ordeals, sharing in the campaigns, the battles, the captivities, the escapes, but none recounted any aspect of these activities in the level of detail that Lamb did.

This book is a compilation of all of Roger Lamb's writings that describe his own life and experiences, most of which focus on his military career. He wrote much more—indeed, most of his surviving writings are about things other than his own life—so this abridgement serves as a convenient source for the information that is unique to him.

THE WRITINGS OF ROGER LAMB

During his career as a soldier, Roger Lamb apparently kept a journal, taught others to read and write, and penned profuse amounts of military paperwork. Only one document written by him while he was in the army is known to survive. After his second escape from captivity, he submitted an intelligence report to the commander in chief with the whimsical title, "Journal of three serjeants of the 23rd Regiment, who made their escape from York, in Pennsylvania." It chronicled much of his time as an escapee in late 1781 and early 1782, with particular focus on the Loyalist citizens who helped him and his comrades. The report is in the Sir Henry Clinton Papers at the William L. Clements Library; a transcript of the entire report appears in the appendix of this volume.

Decades later Lamb wrote that he completed and signed discharge forms for his fellow soldiers in 1784, but none of these papers are known to survive. The large collection of discharges held in The National Archives begins with those prepared in 1785.

Lamb went before the army pension examining board on March 8, 1784, but was denied a pension because he was still in good health and was still capable of earning a living. In 1809 Lamb petitioned for an army pension, submitting two letters describing highlights of his service; both letters survive in the National Archives of Great Britain. Lamb included copies of both letters in one of his books, and they appear in Chapter 11 of this volume.

Lamb's first book, *An Original and Authentic Journal of Occurrences during the late American War, from its commencement to the year 1783*, was published in Dublin in 1809. Its reprinting in 1968 brought it widespread notice, and it remains the best-known and most widely-used narrative of a British enlisted man during the American Revolution. As a resource the book has its shortcomings. Lamb composed it not as a personal journal but as a history of the war, beginning with the political turmoil of the 1760s. Many chapters are devoted to topics to which Lamb had no first-hand exposure, from the establishment of the Continental Congress to General

William Howe's campaigns from 1776 through 1778. It is clear that the author—perhaps guided by his publisher—took an approach that he hoped would make the book more appealing to the market than an autobiography might be. The material is reasonably accurate, and when it was published it may have been a useful reference, but for modern historians Lamb's accounts of things he did not experience, which take up about three quarters of the book, have no value. The important material is his account of his own participation in the war: his voyage from Cork to Quebec in 1776, participation in the campaigns from Canada in 1776 and 1777, participation in the 1781 campaign in the Carolinas and Virginia, and especially his detailed accounts of his two escapes from captivity in 1778 and 1781-82. Useful though this material is, it is interspersed with the more general history of the war, making it difficult to use. In the 438-page book, only 95 pages describe Lamb's own experiences.

In 1811 Lamb published a second book, *Memoir of his Own Life*. His intention was clearly stated in the introduction: "the plan of his American Journal precluded him from detailing many matters intimately connected with Trans-atlantic hostilities, which, he flatters himself, his Memoir introduces of course and with propriety." Detail them he did, but similar to *An Original and Authentic Journal*, much of the work is not about Lamb's own experience, but about disparate topics that he considered important. In an apparent attempt to capitalize on the popularity of travel literature that was an important part of the publishing market during the latter half of the eighteenth and early nineteenth centuries, Lamb's second book is filled with descriptions and histories of many American localities, local legends, and anecdotes of historical figures. The book includes extensive passages copied verbatim from other sources, properly attributed but not informative. For example, the first three pages concern his childhood, including an incident he had when learning to swim at the age of six; the next twenty-four pages are taken up with recommendations on how to teach swimming, passages by other writers on swimming, lives lost in shipwrecks, and other matters unrelated to the author's own life. In all, only about 75 pages of the 292-page volume record the author's own experiences.

After I published an abridged version of Lamb's two books in 2004, a descendent of Roger Lamb's sister wrote to the publisher asking me to contact him. He was in possession of Lamb's commonplace book, a large volume of miscellaneous writings and drawings. The owner was kind enough to photograph each of its 419 pages so that I could examine them and sort out the important from the trivial. That effort led to the publication of a two-part article featuring details of Roger Lamb's experiences as a British soldier that were not included in his books. The owner has since donated the commonplace book to the Methodist Historical Society of Ireland Archive in Belfast, Ireland, which also holds a few letters written by Lamb late in his life.

The commonplace book is a large volume, originally blank, in which Lamb recorded anything that he wanted to remember. Most pages feature a picture and a few words or a paragraph about it—information on nature, on science, on history. Surrounding these central images are bits of writing in every direction filling all of the available space, only occasionally related to the picture. Inspirational quotations, spiritual musings, anecdotes, couplets and short verses, fill page after page, some in cursive, some in block lettering. Here and there are passages describing specific experiences as a soldier or events later in life.

Many pages feature verbatim passages from *An Original and Authentic Journal*, accompanied by an illustration. Whoever drew and colored these pictures rendered them in such a stylized manner that they have little value as depictions of the actual events. The soldiers are clothed in styles of the early 1800s rather than in the uniforms of the 1770s and 1780s. Fortifications in America appear as stone castles rather than the earth and wood structures that most were. To the historian the illustrations tell nothing.

Among the thousands of disparate musings in the commonplace book are a few passages that add to Lamb's other writings about his life and experiences. In a few cases passages in the commonplace book differ from similar passages in *An Original and Authentic Journal*, in ways that suggest judicious editing to avoid exposing controversial material. For example, soon after the 9th Regiment of Foot set out through the wilderness south of Lake Champlain to seek out Fort Anne, they "overtook some boats laden with baggage, women and invalids, belonging to the Americans," which they "immediately secured" according to the published *Journal*. In his private commonplace book, Lamb recounted the event somewhat differently, writing, "The woods being very thick hid the creek from our view and the whole Regiment was ordered to fire a volley near the place where the noise of the oars were heard; the boats stopped immediately. Two ladies were wounded one of them through her breasts and brought on shore."

There are significant differences between Lamb's "Journal of three serjeants of the 23rd Regiment, who made their escape," written immediately after the escape in 1782, and his account of the escape in *An Original and Authentic Journal* published in 1809, presumably written during that decade, over twenty years after the event. A more detailed comparison reveals that the differences are mostly in chronology—Lamb's recollection of the sequence of events changed, along with many details, but in general the *Journal* records all of the same events as Lamb's 1782 account. Here and there in the *Journal* and *Memoir* Lamb named officers and soldiers he served with, all of which correlate with military records. It is possible that Lamb exaggerated or elaborated on his experiences to provide an entertaining narrative, but enough of his recollections are verifiable that his writings can be considered reliable.

In the 1940s, British novelist Robert Graves adapted Lamb's books into a pair of novels entitled *Sergeant Lamb of the Ninth* (London: Methuen, 1940; also released as *Sergeant Lamb's America*, New York: Random House, 1940) and *Proceed, Sergeant Lamb* (London: Methuen, 1941; New York: Random House, 1941). Graves paraphrased some passages from Lamb's books, and explained in his introduction that he did not alter the character of any individuals named by Lamb; that is, when Graves needed villainous characters, he used men who Lamb described as having gotten into trouble, and so forth. But Graves' works are purely novels. He created interactions between characters, love interests, and subplots that do not exist in Lamb's own writing. Nonetheless, some have interpreted Graves' introductory comments to mean that he faithfully retold Lamb's stories, leading to some of Graves' writing being taken as Lamb's.

ABOUT THIS BOOK

This book is an abridgment of Roger Lamb's *Journal* and *Memoir*. Passages from his commonplace book have been added and are indicated by footnotes. "Sources" in the endmatter lists the pages from the two published books and the commonplace book used for this volume. For the most part the two books discuss different phases of Lamb's career, so combining them into a single narrative was a simple matter of piecing them together. In a few places, blending material from the two sources required slight changes from Lamb's original wording.

Spelling, punctuation and italicization are as in the original documents, including blatant spelling and grammatical errors. In a very few places, individual words have been added so that sentences from the different sources blend together properly. Lamb's variations in style, including the intermittent use of dated journal entries and the copying or adaptation of passages from other works, have been preserved. The headings summarizing each chapter's contents have been abridged from the originals; the chapter titles and the numbering of the chapters are new to this volume.

The material in this book is focused on Roger Lamb's military service. The final chapter includes a series of passages from the commonplace book that recount specific events in Lamb's later life. General knowledge of two major campaigns is helpful: the 1777 campaign to Saratoga led by Gen. John Burgoyne, and the 1781 campaign through the Carolinas to Virginia led by Gen. Charles, Earl Cornwallis. “Recommended Reading” in the endmatter lists books on the lives of British soldiers, the campaigns that Lamb served in, and his postwar life as a schoolmaster in Dublin.

CHAPTER ONE

[Early Life in Dublin]

Notices why individuals made Memoirs of their Lives. Author's parentage. His inclination for a Seafaring life. Learns to Swim. Author's constant predilection for going to Sea. His Father tries to dissuade from it, by taking him to behold four Seamen hung in Gibbets. Author accompanies a Mr. Howard on a visit to the Country. Author, on his return to Dublin endeavours to go with the Son of Mr. William Howard to America. Being disappointed he enters on board a Vessel going to that Country. Is persuaded by his Father to forego the Voyage he intended. Author tries to know the use of the Small Sword.

VARIOUS ARE THE CAUSES which induced individuals to commit the incidents of their own lives to writing, and submit them to the world. Vanity has urged several to publish transactions which had been much better reserved in secret, as matters of repentance and motives to amendment. Avarice has stimulated others, to fabricate tissues of falsehood, palatable to the public taste, but exceedingly injurious to unwary readers. Party and prejudice have had no small share in private memoirs; whilst even religion itself has been so misconceived by weak, though well meaning persons, as to furnish a leading inducement for laying before mankind an indiscreet exposure of their lives and actions, which ultimately proved deeply detrimental to the solid interests of piety and truth.

Fully aware of these powerful objections, the author ruminated much before he ventured to add one to the number of those who have published their own biography. But when he recollects what he was, when he feels what the Almighty has done for him, when he balances his present comforts against his past transgressions, when he thinks on the probability that his example may not be altogether without its moral and spiritual utility, when he considers the misrepresentations and falsehoods that have gone abroad relative to the important affairs in which he was personally engaged—the many exalted characters under whom he served in the army, and the facts concerning them, of which he is in possession; when he knows that the experience of his life supplies a plentiful harvest of interesting anecdote, he believes he does not assert too much when he declares, that he should hold himself inexcusable to his king, his country, his officers, the public, and himself, if he suffered the grave to close for ever on his story, without leaving some memorial behind him. These considerations induced him to publish a life, in which he has many things to deplore, and more to call forth his gratitude both to heaven and earth.

I drew my first breath in the city of Dublin, on the 17th of January, 1756, of humble, industrious, and virtuous parents. I was the youngest of eleven children. My eldest brother sacrificed his life in defence of his country: he died in consequence of a wound which he received on board one of the king's ships. At the time of his death I was only five years old; but I remember that my father was greatly afflicted at it: and the more so, when he found my inclination of mind was also to the sea. Considering his situation, which though reputable, was far from affluent, and the labour necessary to support his family; he was a man of much reading, which strong native powers of intellect had led him to digest and methodize. He was far from being unacquainted with seafaring matters. I well remember, when a child, walking with him down the North Wall, he would describe to me, in the most easy and interesting manner, a naval engagement, and by the most apt and familiar transition, turn the discourse to the battles which were then fighting between the English and the French. I am aware that my father's motive, while he amused me in these conversations, was to instruct: but he little imagined, that in so doing, he was kindling a martial ardor in my young breast, which might, and ultimately did lead my heedless steps into the very dangers he would have wished me to shun, and against which he would have guarded me with the fondest anxiety. At length he began to perceive his error: for when he discovered my attention engrossed by these subjects, with tears in his eyes, he would say, "Ah, my dear child, I see your little breast is fired with this account. I only relate these things to inform your judgment. I have lost one fine boy already in fighting for his Country. Surely you will never leave your father. You must stay with me and your mother; and be our support and comfort in our old days." Much as I loved my father, and deep as these affectionate speeches sunk in my mind; they had a tendency which he little imagined when he first used them. It was from these discourses of my father that an anxious desire was first raised in my mind for a seafaring life.

Our house being contiguous to the river Liffey, I was a constant frequenter of its quays, and the places where the shipping were moored. There I soon acquired the art of climbing up the masts of the vessels. At the age of six years I began to practice the art of swimming; but by my temerity, I was near losing my life at that tender period. This circumstance occurred in the old dock, near the spot where the new Custom-house now stands. The tide was full in, and, in imitation of some grown lads, who practised these leaps, as feats of activity, I jumped from off the steps. I soon, however found, that what I had before thought swimming, in shallow water, was but the paddling of a child: for I sunk like a stone, in nearly ten feet of water. Among the spectators, providentially for me, were many expert swimmers; one of whom observing that I did not rise to the surface of the water, immediately plunged in, and took me up, almost dead. This circumstance, far from deterring me from going again into the water, only made me more eager to acquire perfection in the art of swimming, in which, after some time, I became such a proficient, that, from off the bowsprits and round-tops of ships, I frequently leaped head foremost into the river. I now recollect the dangers to which I exposed myself on the watery element, even before I had attained my ninth year! I recognize with gratitude, the protecting arm divine, and, in humble adoration of that Providence which has hitherto guided me in safety, through the progress of an eventful life, am led to say with the poet,

"Oft hath the sea confest thy pow'r,
And given me back to thy command
It could not, Lord! my life devour,
Safe in the hollow of thy hand."[1]

I had not yet attained my eighth year; nevertheless such was my predilection in favour of a seafaring life, that it did not escape the observation of my father. He was much grieved at the discovery, and frequently laid before me in the most fond and anxious manner the distresses and dangers to which sailors are exposed. Giddy, unthinking, bent on marine pursuits, this had little effect on me. However, a circumstance happened at that time in Dublin*, which in a great degree turned my mind against its favourite pursuit. It was as follows, I have mentioned that it was the usage of my father to walk with me on the banks of the Liffey, and the quays of the harbour. In one of these amusing and instructive little rambles which my affectionate parent always tried to turn to my advantage, he carried me (no doubt on purpose) along the South-wall, and near the Pigeon-house, in the direction of the Light-house, where at present the wall is extended by that strong and beautiful work which adds so greatly to the advantage and ornament of the city. Here were hung in chains, on gibbets, four criminals, whose dreadful offence almost appears to have called down the avenging hand of Divine

*In the year 1766.

1. From Hymn 289, *A Collection of Hymns for the People Called Methodists*, Rev. John Wesley, London, 1780.

justice itself, to arrest and exhibit them, as terrible examples to individuals in general. They were purposely exposed in the mouth of the harbour as a warning to seafaring men. The exposure, and the whole circumstance of the affair proved a powerful dissuasive to prevent me, at that time, from entertaining the desire which before engaged my thoughts. I no longer wished for the sea.

When I was eleven years of age, I began to entertain a strong desire to leave home. My father, ever anxious to comply with my wishes, yielded to an offer which presented itself, and consented that I should go with a friend of his to the country. This proposal was joyfully received by me, and preparations were accordingly made for my departure to the north of Ireland.

The gentleman who took charge of me, was going to visit his sister a Mrs. Hinds, near Killishandra, in the county of Cavan, and some other relations which he had in the county of Westmeath. But it was to his uncle, who was my father's great friend, that I was principally indebted on that occasion. On my father's application, he recommended me to his nephew, with the warmth of a friend, and the authority of a parent. This gentleman, whose name was Howard, was a respectable merchant in Jervis-Street. He was a man well acquainted with the world and all its vanities, which he happily forsook for the more solid enjoyments of religion, and the more laudable pursuit of virtue.

Having stopped six weeks in the country, with the nephew of Mr. William Howard, and being much gratified with the tour, from the new scenes which it afforded, interesting to a young mind like mine, I returned to Dublin. On my arrival in town, my attention became greatly occupied in expectation of going to North America, in company with Mr. Howard's son,[2] who had obtained a commission in a marching regiment, which was serving there. I besought my father to intercede with young Mr. Howard to take me along with him.

2. Francis Howard, commissioned as an ensign in the 18th Regiment of Foot in December 1767; he drowned near Fort Chartres in Illinois in 1771. Steven M. Baule, *Protecting the Empire's Frontier: Officers of the 18th (Royal Irish) Regiment of Foot during its North American Service, 1767-1776* (Athens, OH: Ohio University Press, 2014), 185-186.

But, although my indulgent parent agreed in compliance with my ardent wishes, to mention the matter to Mr. Howard, there could be no situation procured in the regiment for a boy such as I then was. I was obliged therefore to remain at home, and the disappointment very much distressed me. But I resolved at all events to depart for America, and, in pursuance of my determination, I seized an opportunity which soon offered, of entering on board a vessel destined for that part of the world. However, my father being apprised of my purpose, interfered with the captain of the ship, paid my expenses on board, and so prevented my intended plan of folly for a time.

I remained at home a disappointed idler, and like most boys who have not received the advantage, the unspeakable advantage, of a truly religious education, became delighted with every folly that but too fatally captivate the juvenile mind. Did youth but seriously consider half the snares and temptations to which they are exposed, they would perceive, that early industry and a constant application to business are, under the divine guidance, their best preservatives.

At that period, the administration of justice was greatly relaxed in the city of Dublin. It was almost impossible for persons to walk through some parts of the city (particularly on Sunday evenings) without encountering the most violent, and sometimes dangerous assaults. Lower Abbey, and Marlborough streets, on the north side of the city, and the Long lane near Kevin-street on the south, were the places for general rendezvous for "Club-law,"[3] as it was vulgarly called. Here numbers of daring, desperate follows, used to assemble, form themselves in battle array, and cut and maim each other without either mercy or remorse.

Whether influenced by these scenes of personal contest, or from a natural and inherent love of a military life, I will not presume to determine; but at this early period of my life, the small-sword exercise became a favourite pursuit. But not meeting with a sufficient number of adversaries to exhibit my skill and keep my hand in practice, this in its turn, became abandoned.

3. "Club-law," rules of the street enforced with clubs.

CHAPTER TWO

[Service as a Soldier in Ireland]

Author inlists in the 9th Regiment of Foot. Acquires a knowledge of Discipline. Suffers great privations by means of a Non-commissioned Officer who had charge of him. Desertions were mediated in consequence of such abuses; but through fear, the men forbore to take so rash a step. Author much terrified at seeing a man flogged for Desertion. Hon. Geo. Rawdon (brother to the Earl of Moira) joins the Regiment. Account of Major Bolton. Author by means of bad company falls into snares in Waterford. The Author marches with his Regiment for the North of Ireland. Is quartered at Downpatrick. Ordered to Saintfield. Dissipation of the privates there.

SERJEANT LAMB'S SKETCH OF HIMSELF IN HIS YOUTH

Before I was 18 years of age, I enrolled myself among the defenders of my King and Country and passed in a few years through the several grades of military office to that of pay master Serjeant. I delighted to gird myself with the armory of death and was proud to appear in military decorations. As to my person I was about five feet nine inches. I had a cadaverous countenance full of cavities and projections and a body as thin, and straight as a lath, and in spite of the meekness of my name I was neither gentle by nature nor polished by education, I was rough and active with the voice of a lion, and a long black head of hair tied behind. I cannot say I went forward to battle with a fearless heart and destructive arm, but this will I say, that in facing danger both my body and soul were often put into an uproar.[1]

I had now arrived at a remarkable epoch in my life; since it was that which in a great measure gave a cast to its future operations. It was on the 10th of August, 1773, then in my 17th year, when being seduced to gaming by some evil companions, with whom I thoughtlessly associated, I lost my little all. This juvenile stage of existence is truly critical to both sexes. Forgetful of all the moral lessons so anxiously inculcated in my mind by my father, I was blind to my danger, and united with those who became my corrupters, and worst enemies. Afraid to return and tell my father of my indiscretions, who would have rebuked and forgiven me, I shrank from my best hope, parental admonition, and formed the resolution of entering for a soldier. Accordingly I went to one serjeant Jenkins, who kept a public house opposite the lower barrack gate, and enlisted with him for the 9th regiment of foot, which was then stationed in Waterford. On the 24th I joined the regiment, and was put into the hands of a drill serjeant, and taught to walk and step out like a soldier. This at first was a disagreeable task to me. During twenty-one days I was thus drilled four hours each day. However, having at last rectified the most prominent appearance of my awkwardness, I received a set of accoutrements, and a firelock,[2] and was marched every morning from the barrack to the bowling green, near the water-side, to be instructed in the manual exercise.[3]

That instant he becomes the serjeant's care,
His pupil, and his torment, and his jest.
His awkward gait, his introverted toes,
Bent knees, round shoulders, and dejected looks,

1. This paragraph is from the commonplace book.
2. "Firelock," a flintlock musket. Accoutrements consisted of a waistbelt holding a bayonet scabbard and a cartridge box holding eighteen rounds, and a shoulder belt holding a larger cartridge pouch.
3. "manual exercise," the manual of arms for handling the firelock.

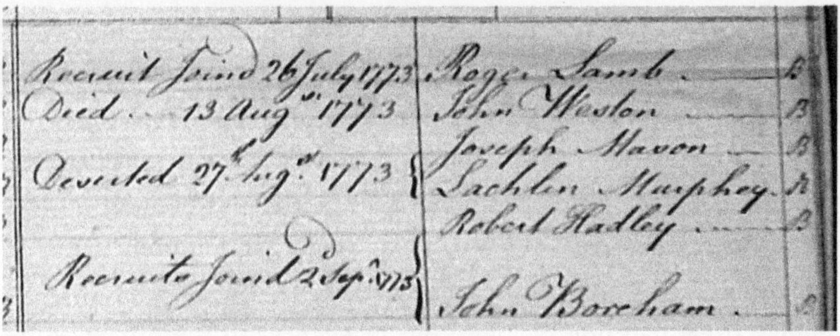
Recruit Joind 26 July 1773 Roger Lamb
Died 13 Augt 1773 John Weston
Joseph Mavon
Deserted 27th Augt 1773 Lachlen Murphey
Robert Hadley
Recruits Joind 2 Sepr 1773 John Boreham

Detail of the muster roll showing Lamb's enlistment into the 9th Regiment of Foot. Lamb recorded the date of his enlistment as August 10, and that he joined the regiment in Waterford on August 24. WO 12/2653, The National Archives.

Procure him many a curse. ————————
Unapt to learn, and form'd of stubborn stuff;
He yet by slow degrees puts off himself,
Grows conscious of a change, and likes it well:
He stands erect, his slouch becomes a walk;
He steps right onward, martial in his air,
His form and movement. ————————[4]

The most disagreeable days of a soldier, are these in which he begins to learn his exercise. And it is seldom that he entertains much regard for those who teach it him. Hence the office of a drill serjeant, although one of the most important is not one of the most thankful. However, without disparaging the soldier's character (an offence of which, I hope, I shall not be thought guilty), I must own that some of the old drill-serjeants were unnecessarily, if not wantonly severe.

Matters changed with me much for the better when I joined my regiment, as far as regarded my personal feelings, but I had to experience other sufferings. I was put into a mess with a number of recruits.[5] The non-commissioned officer who had us in charge received our pay every Saturday, and squandered the greater part of it

4. From *The Task* by William Cowper, 1785.
5. "Mess," a group of five soldiers who received and prepared their provisions as a group.

in paying the expences of his weekly score at the public house, by which means, we had to subsist upon a very scanty allowance, although at that time, provisions were very cheap in Waterford. We often complained in private among ourselves, but whenever we remonstrated with him he menaced us with confinement in the guard-house, and such was our inexperience, and apprehension of being punished by his interference against us, that we submitted in silence. If we had boldly stated our grievances to the officer commanding, we most certainly had been redressed.[6] No doubt such an effect would have resulted from our complaints properly made.

Such ill usage actually proved so oppressive, and nearly intolerable to a party or our men, who were driven almost to abandon the service, that several of them, from continued extortion, and the hardship owing to it, actually conspired together to desert. Happily, however, for them, after proceeding some short way in pursuance of their plot, they were induced, from apprehension of the danger attending such rashness, or probably from the reviving energy of loyal motives, to return in time, before their intention of quitting the regiment could be known. This salutary determination perhaps was suggested by the confinement of a deserter at that time who had to undergo the sentence of a court-martial. The party alluded to, no doubt dreaded, that if they acted rashly as they at first intended, a similar punishment might soon await themselves. However, on the day subsequent to their returning to the barrack, after resolving to resume their military duties, the unfortunate man who deserted was taken out for punishment, attended by the entire regiment.

This was the first man I saw flogged. Being at that time (as I have already observed) only seventeen years of age, with all the warm youthful emotions operating within me, the spectacle made a lasting impression on my mind. I well remember, during the infliction of his punishment, I cried like a child.

6. This is how the original sentence reads; it probably should read "we most certainly would have been redressed."

The noncommissioned officer who had the charge of us, began to be fearful lest his conduct should be made known to the Captain of the company. He spent less of our pay, and of consequence, we were much better provided. However, he still kept us on very unfair allowance. Indeed it would almost have been impossible for me to have supported life with any degree of comfort, had it not been, that I was employed by a serjeant and his wife to teach their son writing and arithmetic.[7] These people were very kind to me, frequently inviting me to their table; and paying me beside. I had also plenty of writing to do for the various serjeants and corporals, in making out their reports, &c. These employments placed me above that starvation which my unfortunate comrades were compelled to endure. However incredible, it is a fact, that merely through fear of this man we endured all this fraud, without making that representation which must have effectually relieved us: for our commanding officer, Major Bolton,[8] being strictly just as well as humane, would have severely punished any non-commissioned officer, found guilty of defrauding the men.

Major Bolton was born in the city of Dublin, commenced his military life very young, and served with ability in the years 1759, 1760, 1761, and 1762. He held the rank of captain in the 9th regiment of foot, for seventeen years before he obtained a majority.[9] Having fought under him in Canada, during the entire campaign of 1776, I had opportunities of witnessing his gallantry and worth. About the end of that year he was promoted to the Lieut. Colonelcy of the 8th foot, at that time on service in Detroit and Niagra; and having taken the command accordingly, he was as usual, distinguished for spirit, talent, and the attachment of the men. Soon after his being appointed Colonel, lamented by the army and all who knew him, he was unfortunately drowned in the lakes while coming

7. For more on literacy and education in the army, see Don N. Hagist, *Noble Volunteers: the British Soldiers who fought the American Revolution* (Yardley, PA: Westholme, 2020), 35-36, 151-155.
8. Mason Bolton, major in the 9th Regiment of Foot.
9. "Majority," the rank of Major.

down to Montreal.[10] Too much could not be said in praise of Col. Bolton, estimating him in his profession or in society. With all the intrepidity and ardour of the military character, he possessed the most honourable mind and benevolent heart. On the occasion of punishing a man for desertion, of which I before gave some account, the Major attended by the officers of the regiment, came to see the sentence of law-martial enforced. After the third drummer inflicted his twenty-five lashes, (i.e. when the offending soldier had received seventy-five,) Major Bolton, without addressing either the surgeon or officers in attendance, advanced, evidently much affected, to the halberts,[11] in a compassionate manner expostulated with the man concerning the magnitude of his offence, and afterward ordered him to be taken down, remitting the remainder of the intended punishment, on the on the soldier's promise of future good conduct. Such severe inflictions were unusual whenever he commanded: he avoided flogging the men as much as possible, and only resorted to it for those great crimes which required extraordinary coercion. For the common breaches of the military laws and duties, he used to send them some hours of the day to drill, sometimes making them wear the regimental coat turned inside out, in order to exhibit them as examples of ill behaviour and disgrace. They were moreover prevented from going on any command,[12] or mounting the principal guards. On some occasions he confined the ill conducted soldier to his barrack-room, or the guard-house, and when his offence deserved it, the man was condemned to the black-hole,[13] and at times obliged to live on bread and water. In short, his mode of treating the men shewed them his unceasing strictness in preserving order and discipline, as also his fine feelings and dispassionate motives.

10. Bolton drowned on October 31, 1776, when the ship *Ontario* sank in a storm on Lake Ontario.

11. "Halberts," or halberds, pole arms with axe-like heads carried by sergeants. When a man was to be lashed, three halberts were tied together to form a tripod, and the man was tied to them.

12. "On command," on detached duty away from the main body of the regiment.

13. "Black-hole," a solitary confinement cell that allowed no light inside.

Private soldier of the 9th Regiment of Foot, as he may have looked in Dublin in 1775. His coat, waistcoat and breeches have been tailored to fit snugly. Black canvas gaiters keep debris out of his shoes and protect the knees of the breeches; black garters secure the tops. The red coat's yellow lapels, cuffs and collar are buttoned back to make it open and airy, as are the skirts of the coat. His bayonet, just out of view on his left side, hangs from a whitened leather waistbelt; a brass buckle bears the number of the regiment. A black leather cartridge pouch hangs on his right hip, held by a broad white belt of soft leather, to which is fastened a small pick and brush for cleaning the musket's firing mechanism. His black broad-brimmed felt hat is folded, or cocked, in the prevalent military style of the era. Illustration by Eric Schnitzer.

While our regiment continued as I before described, commanded by Major Bolton (in 1774) the Hon. George Rawdon, brother to the Earl of Moira, joined it, and was appointed to the command of our company. He was then a promising young officer, and served afterward with distinguished credit under General Burgoyne, until the surrender of our army at Saratoga. At my return from North America, he was Major in a marching regiment quartered in Dublin, and recognized me with that urbanity and amiable attention, for which his family by all ranks are admired. Major Rawdon soon after died of a fever, greatly regretted by his acquaintance.[14]

The biographist who is governed by truth has sometimes a very painful task to perform: he has to narrate circumstances which he could wish never to have happened; or having occurred, to have their remembrance for ever buried from human observation.

During our stay at Waterford I fell into many irregularities. But whatever excuse might be made for me and my companions, from the peculation by which we suffered, as also our youth and inexperience, the real cause lay deeper; we were all alike aliens to God—breakers of his laws—and slighters, if not open contemners of his ordinances. I thank heaven, those days of transgression are long since gone by; and, I humbly hope, are forgiven: but even now, when I reflect on the actions of my life while quartered in Waterford, the remembrance fills my mind with the deepest sorrow.

In the month of May, 1774, we received the route for the North of Ireland, and marched for our destination accordingly. The company to which I belonged was quartered in the town of Downpatrick. A few days after our arrival there, I was ordered on command in an officer's detachment, to the town of Saintfield, ten miles distant from Belfast. Here a circumstance occurred, which

14. The Honorable George Rawdon, younger brother of the famous Francis, Lord Rawdon, who commanded a corps of Loyalists during the latter half of the American war. George Rawdon was commissioned in the 9th Regiment of Foot in July 1775, but had probably joined the regiment as a volunteer in 1774 to wait for a vacant ensigncy. He died in Dublin in 1800.

though it may appear uninteresting to many, should not pass in silence; because it became dangerous and detrimental to myself at the time, and giving it a place in this publication may prove a mean of cautioning and dissuading men in the army,[15] and the various avocations of life, from perilous and depraving diversions. It is somewhere well observed, that "happy is he who takes care and pursues a right path, by marking the dangers and errors of others." In this way it will not be amiss for me to observe that, having by this time associated myself with card-playing companions, I commenced a professed gambler; and so ardent was my passion for gaming that by my losses at cards, I often brought myself into great difficulties.

Card-playing is often attended, no doubt, with dangerous consequences, when the mind becomes enamoured of the game. The winner proceeds with ideas of avarice, and the loser to recover his losses, and even where money is not risked, as a diversion, playing at cards administers to idleness and dissipation.

"Cards are superfluous, with all the tricks
That idleness has ever yet contriv'd,
To fill the void of an unfurnish'd brain,
To palliate dullness, and give time a shove."[16]

When I look back at my unguarded and dissipated conduct at that period, I am obliged to pause and bless a kind Providence that I did not, from the precipice on which I then stood, fall into open disgrace and ruin. To supply the expenses of playing, the privates sold their necessaries[17] and squandered their pay. Many did even worse; and it is really matter of wonder, how they evaded detection, when the officers inspected and reviewed the state of their necessaries. On such occasions they frequently borrowed shirts, shoes,

15. This is how the original sentence reads; it probably should read "may prove a means of cautioning."
16. From a work by William Cowper.
17. "Necessaries," articles of clothing provided to a soldier on an as-needed basis, namely, shirts, shoes and stockings. Other uniform items, such as the coat, waistcoat and breeches, were issued annually.

stockings and other articles of regimental appointment from their comrades, who happened to be absent on guard, while the inspection and scrutiny took place. In this manner they frequently eluded strict examination. Once, an affair occurred, which had it been detected, would have deservedly exposed the individual to severe punishment. It was as follows: it is notorious that soldiers in most quarters, can without difficulty find wives; but in the north of Ireland, wherever the regiment was stationed, young women appeared to have a predilection for our men, and it being expected that we would shortly be sent to serve in America, the commanding officer issued a general order to prevent them from marrying without a written permission, signed by the officers of the company or detachment; and even the ministers of the place were desired not to solemnize the marriages of soldiers without consulting the officers, and having such military licenses, as but a few young women could be taken on board when the regiment embarked for foreign service.[18] While this prevention was enforced, a soldier belonging to our detachment made a contract, and despairing of obtaining permission to marry, he prevailed on another to counterfeit the signature of his officer. The curate of the place was imposed on, and the soldier was married. And although Lieutenant Sweetman,[19] who commanded at Saintfield endeavoured to find out the person who counterfeited his name, the man escaped an exposure; the consequence of which would have been attended with certain and just punishment. Whether or not Lieutenant Sweetman scrutinized in so strict a manner as he might, I cannot determine. Probably he was not displeased in his not having occasion to punish an individual in a manner sufficient to terrify others from committing such a transgression. Had it been ascertained, punishment of course could not have been avoided.

18. The War Office allocated shipping space for 60 wives with each British regiment, but other wives sometimes obtained their own passage.
19. George Swettenham, a lieutenant in the 9th Regiment of Foot.

CHAPTER THREE

[Voyage to America]

Author returns with his Regiment to Dublin. Is made Corporal by Lord Ligonier, the Colonel. New Exercise. State of Newgate Jail at that time, and of the City Watch. Author embarks for North America. Sails from the Cove of Cork. Remarkable Occurrences during the Voyage. Arrives at Quebec.

In the beginning of the year 1775, our regiment was ordered for Dublin duty, and Lord Ligonier, the colonel,[1] arrived from England to inspect and take the command of it. His Lordship was generous, humane, and, from the excellency of his mind, and the affability of his manners, was greatly beloved by the men in general. Some time after his having joined the regiment, I was by him promoted to be a corporal, and sent among several other non-commissioned officers to be instructed in the new exercise which shortly before had been introduced by General Sir William Howe. It consisted of a set of manœuvres for light infantry, and was ordered by his Majesty to be practised in the different regiments. To make trial of this excellent mode of discipline for light troops, and render it general without delay, seven companies were assembled at Salisbury in the summer of 1774. His Majesty himself went to Salisbury to

1. Lord Edward Ligonier, colonel of the 9th Regiment of Foot.

see them, and was much pleased with their utility, and the manner of their execution. The manœuvres were chiefly intended for woody and intricate districts, with which North America abounds, where an army cannot act in line. The light infantry manœuvres made use of at present are different from those of Sir William Howe, which were done from centre of battalions, grand divisions, and sub-divisions, by double Indian files.[2] They were six in number, and well adapted for the service in America. Our regiment was instructed in them by the 33d, at that time quartered in Dublin, and commanded by Lord Cornwallis. The 33d was in a high state of appointment, and exceedingly well disciplined, by that able disciplinarian Colonel Webster.[3] I never witnessed any regiment that excelled it in discipline and military appearance. The men mounted guard in a superior style. Each centinal, during the two hours he remained on his post, continued always in motion, and could not walk less than seven miles in that time. The soldier was ever alert and alive in attention; when on duty—all eye—all ear. Even in the centry-box, which the centinal never entered unless when it rained, he was not allowed to keep the palm of his hand carelessly on the muzzle of his firelock, which, if the piece were loaded, was considered dangerous, and always an awkward attitude for the soldier. This soldierly character they always maintained while they served in North America. The Royal Welch fuzileers[4] were brigaded with the 33d during the entire of the campaign in South Carolina; both regiments were well united together, and furnished an example for cleanliness, martial spirit, and good behaviour. This in a great measure was owing to the care and attention of their Colonels, who were unremitting in trying to make their men excel in discipline, duty, and general propriety of conduct. In effecting this military excellence of our Brigade, Colonel

2. For details on these maneuvers, see Don N. Hagist, *These Distinguished Corps: British Grenadier and Light Infantry Battalions in the American Revolution* (Helion, 2021).
3. James Webster, lieutenant colonel of the 33rd Regiment of Foot.
4. The 23rd Regiment of Foot, Royal Welch Fusiliers. Lamb used the spellings "fusileers" and "fuzileers."

(now General) Nesbit Balfour,[5] who commanded the Royal Welch fuzileers, deserved great credit, and when he was removed to the important situation of Commandant at Charlestown, the men sustained a loss; for it should be mentioned to his honour as an officer, that during his short stay with us, the regiment was much improved, so much so, that we were not in any thing inferior to the 33d. It is here not unworthy of remark to observe, that both in war and peace, the state of the regiment in every military point of view, and even in good morals, depends on the exertion and ability of the officer commanding, by whom the men are kept regular, steady, vigilant, and active in all cases.

After I had acquired a knowledge of the new discipline from the non-commissioned officers of the 33d regiment, I was appointed to take charge of a squad[6] of our regiment, and executed that important and laborious task to the best of my ability. The constant attendance and habit of exercise is almost every thing in the soldier's life; and it is indeed surprising to see how soon an awkward young man becomes well disciplined, performs his evolutions with a neat agility, and handles his arms with a graceful dexterity. The soldier who is able to carry and handle his arms and go through his manual exercise without letting fall a crown piece which is placed between his elbow and his side—I think understands his exercise.[7] In the acquisition of these soldierly requisites, the drill-serjeant of course, is chiefly instrumental; and therefore his unceasing industry and faithfulness are indispensable. In performing the necessary business of the drill, I was constant and careful; by which activity and usefulness I obtained the good will and esteem of my officers, particularly of

5. Nesbit Balfour, lieutenant-colonel of the 23rd Regiment, was for a time commander of the British post at Ninety-Six in South Carolina, and later of the city of Charlestown (today Charleston).

6. "Squad," or squad of inspection, a group of ten to twenty men supervised by a non-commissioned officer. The purpose of the squad was to promote proper discipline, and proper care of clothing and equipment; it was not a tactical or operational organization. See Hagist, *Noble Volunteers*, 40-41.

7. This sentence is from the commonplace book.

Colonel Taylor,[8] who commanded at that time the 9th regiment, and also of Major Bolton, who ever afterwards while he stopped with the regiment befriended me. My employment of drilling the men did not preclude me from the performance of other duties. I mounted guard in turn, and at one time, in 1775, was appointed for the Newgate guard. At that time the Jail of Newgate was a small mean building, and in no degree suited to the respectability of a great city. It stood on the site of ground now denominated Corn-market, a short distance from High-street, and contiguous to Thomas-street. It happened in the range of my duty, to have the command of a guard there, upon a Saturday, when a criminal, pursuant to the sentence of the law, was to be taken from the prison to be hung at Gallows-green, at that time the usual place of similar executions. On this occasion considerable crowds collected in the adjoining streets and lanes, which, considering the local situation of the jail, proved inconvenient and very alarming to the guard. The mob assembled in such numbers that the narrow and confined arch leading into Thomas-street, was completely filled with people; and having but twelve men, a corporal and myself, I apprehended a rescue, as I could not confide much in the assistance of the city watchmen; they being in general infirm and altogether unfit for that severe and dangerous duty, which must occasionally devolve on the peace officers and body of the police. However, I disposed of my little guard as cautiously and ably as I could; and the High Sheriffs of the city behaved with such circumspection and spirit on the occasion, that the mob was overawed, and the criminal's cart moved through High-street without any molestation being offered to the watch, who then always attended on such occasions, or making it necessary for the guard to fire, as it was suspected at first we would be under the necessity of doing.

A circumstance which happened at another time of my mounting guard at the jail will shew what daring attempts used to be then

8. William Taylor, lieutenant-colonel of the 9th Regiment of Foot.

made, and also the severe responsibility which attached to the guard on such a duty. It was afterwards found that a culprit named Cunningham, a noted highwayman, conspired with some other prisonners to escape from confinement on this night, but whether it was that their plan was not enough matured, or that they feared the guard, they postponed the meditated attempt until the next night. Unfortunately for the serjeant who relieved me, they succeeded in the following manner. On the stairs was a door leading down to the hall, in which were two apartments, one used as a tap-room, and the other occupied by a man called Meaghan, who was employed in the two-fold capacity of turnkey and hangman. The door on the stairs, when locked, secured all the prisoners, but an usuage was permitted, viz. to indulge two or three prisoners together, to regale in the tap-room, if they were supplied with money to pay for the refreshments they called for. It was a custom with the confined then as well as now, to beg from people passing the jail, by making loud appeals to the pity of individuals, and letting down a bag through the grated windows to receive alms; and the collections thus acquired afforded a fund for the expenditure of the tap-room, at least to some of the culprits.

The use of the taproom suggested to the fertile invention of the culprit Cunningham a scheme which he concerted with two others. Having contrived to saw their iron bolts nearly through, Cunningham accompanied by one of them, asked for leave to go and take punch before the door on the stairs was finally closed for the night. Leave given, they proceeded to the room, asked for spirits, and while his comrade discoursed with the centinel, who had but a bayonet on his post, Cunningham broke off his bolts, and knocked the soldier down. The turnkey's wife (her husband lying sick of a fever in the room adjoining) rushed in on hearing the noise, and was seized by Cunningham, and his associate who strove to force the keys from her. After a struggle, which she resisted for nearly half an hour, before they could take the key of the door on the stairs, they admitted their companion down through the door which they then locked, and next proceeded to oblige the turnkey's wife to give the remaining key. The woman, although severely beaten and bruised continued to refuse, and made the most astonishing resistance. She endeavoured, with calling aloud, to alarm the guard, fastened the key in her clothes, which she did not let go until some of the joints of her fingers were broken, and she had been much injured from the blows she received, and was at last left entirely exhausted. By this time the guard from the cries of the woman, were alarmed and drawn up before the outer door, which (notwithstanding the obstacle of an iron chain fastened diagonally across, and other strong precautions) they unlocked, and what was more amazing, effected their escape in the face of the guard, by running away through Towns Arch without being at all maimed, or receiving the slightest wound. This most extraordinary success of ruffian hardihood, no doubt emboldened Cunningham to resume his career of robbery on the roads; by which he put himself in the way of being again imprisoned, and making that capital atonement with his guilty life to often offended justice, which sooner or later is generally found to be the catastrophe of such incorrigible and inhuman offenders.[9]

The escaping of the prisoners proved disgraceful to the serjeant on duty, who together with his guard, was confined for it. I felt a cordial satisfaction, when I reflected that this jail-breaking conspiracy was intended to take place on the day before, when I mounted guard. But it did not make that impression of thankfulness on me which it ought.

I was again seduced into habits of dissipation and idleness, which gradually proved instrumental in rendering me less esteemed by my officers, who, previously were induced in consequence of my generally correct behaviour to think well of me. Serjeant Clarke and corporal Lamb were put into the Black Hole. After being tried by a court Martial I was brought to the Royal Square barrack in Dublin

9. Thomas Cunningham was committed to prison in June 1775 for robbery; he escaped in August and was recaptured and tried in October. *Saunders's News-Letter* (Dublin), June 28, October 16 and 23, 1775; *Hibernian Journal* (Dublin), August 30, 1775.

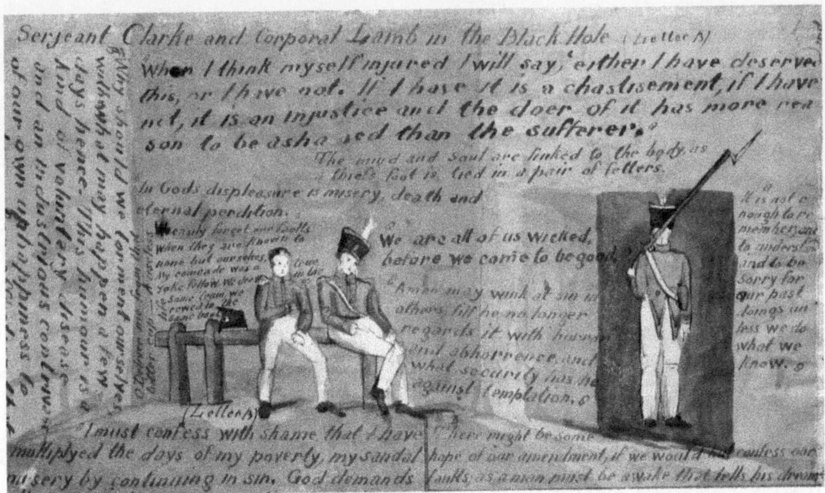

Lamb's commonplace book includes this illustration of himself and Sergeant Sampson Clarke confined for an unspecified infraction in Dublin in 1775. Like all of the commonplace book illustrations, the uniforms are typical of the early 1800s rather than the 1770s. Lamb made no mention of this incident in his published books. Methodist Historical Society of Ireland.

to receive my sentence, October 1775. Adjutant Fife read the sentence of the court martial. He concluded in these words. "The court having taken into consideration the several charges preferred against corporal Lamb do find him guilty and is therefore sentenced to be reduced to the ranks. Drum Major do your duty"—The drum major then cut off my shoulder knott and I was sent into the ranks. I was twenty years of age at this time.[10]

I was seized with severe sickness in January, 1776; and being sent into the general military hospital in James'-street, (at present used as barracks), I was disabled to march with our regiment on its receiving the route to proceed to Cork and embark for North America. I was the only soldier of the 9th obliged to stop behind in

10. This passage, from "Serjeant Clarke" to the end of the paragraph, is from the commonplace book with text adapted to fit the narrative. Lamb did not record the charges against him. Sergeant Sampson Clarke retained his rank through the last available muster rolls prepared in February 1777. Muster rolls, 9th Regiment of Foot, WO 12/2653, The National Archives, Kew, UK (TNA).

Dublin. The departure of the regiment was a source of regret, which made me anxious for health and strength to follow and embark with it for the American Continent. On the 3d of March, 1776, I thought myself enough recovered to leave the hospital, as I did, and without loss of time waited on Sir William Montgomery, our army agent,[11] in Mary-street. Here I was informed, that the regiment was supposed to be on its voyage, and it was recommended to me to join the additional company belonging to us, employed in England on the recruiting service.[12] My relations were urgent with me to go and stop with the recruiting parties, in order to detain me from the dangers of foreign service. But I considered that remaining aloof from it in a season of warfare did not consist with the spirit and manhood of a soldier. I resolved that I would not sit down indulging myself in the sunshine of peace and inactivity in the British islands, while my brethren and friends in arms were in the progress of fighting the battles of their king and country on distant shores. At all events I determined to repair to the Cove of Cork, and sail if possible, along with our regiment. In the event of my arriving too late to do so, I was purposed to take my passage in some ship bound to Quebec, that I might have an opportunity of partaking in the honourable dangers which my fellow-soldiers had to undertake. While I was about leaving Dublin, a recruit for the regiment from Downpatrick was sent by our army agent, that I might take charge of him. I was glad at finding an additional man for our ranks, and, he being in the need of clothes and other necessaries, I furnished him as well as I was able, and also advanced him a fortnight's pay, knowing I should be refunded whatever I thus gave him. I found a place to lodge him at night, desiring him to have every thing prepared next day for our intended journey to Cork. I called on the morning fol-

11. "Agent," a private accountant or accounting firm that handled a regiment's finances.
12. On August 25, 1775, the War Office authorized each regiment on service in America (or ordered thereto) to form two "Additional Companies" for recruiting in the Britain and Ireland. These were companies in name only, and served as vehicles for the funding of recruitment activities.

lowing, but lo! our unfledged hero was flown. I was angry, and anxious that he should not have any cause to plume himself by *running the old soldier* so much to my expense, I put up placards in the most public parts of the city, advertising the deserter, and minutely describing his person, age, and every particular whereby I thought he might be taken. And I had the satisfaction to be instrumental in his apprehension; which was effected soon after on the Drogheda road, from whence he was sent under a guard of soldiers to the Cove of Cork, in time to embark with our men to America.

After making arrangements to arrest our run-away recruit, on the 6th of March, 1776, I took a mournful farewell of my fond parents and friends in Dublin. The scene of parting between humble but virtuous parents and the child of their affections, going on such a destination as I was then about to pursue, awakens sharp sensations which search the soul, and seem to strain the ties of nature! A poor father beholds his beloved offspring going from his lowly roof (probably never to return) and most sensibly laments that want of competence which might keep his youthful family to prop his old age at home. The son himself (although his spirit is buoyant on the wings of expectation, and his foot is pressing forward in the step of inexperience!) pauses in the warm embrace of his weeping parent, and regrets that he ever indulged the wandering idea of forsaking domestic endearment and peace. The painful ceremony of separation in such a case, although it operates in a tumult of tenderness, faithfully exhibits the true satisfactions of our fluctuating lives—impressing us with a living seal of sorrow, that when we abandon the bosom of early affection and friendship, we leave our most precious pleasures behind us, and that home is the asylum of happiness on earth.

A melancholy cloud hung on me at leaving my parents and native place, but youth and hope soon brightened my face, and induced me to think the labour of walking light. Thus, after being so long delayed by the pressure of sickness, I arrived at the Cove of Cork a fortnight before the regiment embarked. My valuable friend, Major

Bolton expressed himself pleased at my joining the regiment of which he then had the command on its going abroad. Major Bolton's welcome for me was increased from his being aware that I was indeed a volunteer going to America, as I might have stopped with the recruiting parties. He therefore immediately promoted me in his own company.[13] At the same time Surgeon Lindsay asked Major Bolton to permit me to go and assist in attending the sick, as there was then but a single Surgeon in the regiment.[14] But I became so useful to himself that he would not comply, promising, however, that when he could better spare me he would accommodate Surgeon Lindsay, by letting him have me. I now had the happiness of being restored to the confidence and esteem of my officers, from whom I received many favours and much kind treatment.

On the 3d of April, 1776, I embarked with the 9th regiment of foot, in which I was then a non-commissioned officer, at the Cove of Cork, on board the Friendship, transport, and on the 8th sailed with the fleet for Quebec. Thus I had much cause of satisfaction at leaving home and embarking for foreign service in a well appointed expedition consisting of the 9th, 20th, 24th, 34th, 53d, and 62d regiments.[15] It was indeed a fine sight to behold 300 sail of transports full of British troops, convoyed by two frigates, proceeding together from Cove with a favourable wind at N. E. As we got out I stood on deck eying my native country with indescribable emotions, as the land was disappearing from my view. It of course occurred to me how probable it was that I might never again return to the embraces of the best of parents whom I had disappointed in their fond hopes respecting me. And although the "circumstance of war," martial music, and ships under weigh arrested my youthful fancy, the idea of being

13. That is, appointed him corporal. Lamb is listed as a private soldier on the regiment's muster rolls until this time. Muster rolls, 9th Regiment of Foot, WO 12/2653, TNA.
14. "Surgeon," the regiment's medical officer; each regiment also had a surgeon's mate. Henry Shelly was appointed surgeon in the 9th Regiment in February 1776.
15. Besides these regiments from Ireland, the expedition included the 21st, 29th and 31st regiments from England.

separated perhaps for ever, from parents, friends, and country, penetrated my bosom with a pang which nothing could remove at the moment. I was sure my father suffered greatly on my account. I was his favourite child, and I have reason to apprehend, that my leaving my parents, and pursuing a perilous line of life, proved somewhat instrumental in accelerating his decease, which took place about two years after I went to serve in America. This thought frequently operated in my heart to render me indeed unhappy. However, it is one of those sad consequences, which attend travelling, that we frequently leave our dearest attachments, and find them gone for ever in this world when we return from our wanderings.

Travelling by sea supplies a variety of scenes and occurrences, which although uninteresting to persons used to them, about with a degree of interest to others, and chiefly young persons. So it happened to the author of this humble work, who even at that early time of his life, indulged reflection a good deal, and while on his passage to America, considered he was going to a world which must be somewhat new and unsuited to the habits and constitution of Europeans. In this idea he commenced a regimen of diet and living which he thought might fit him for the severities of Northern latitudes, and the fatigues of warfare. He of purpose used a sparing diet, took his birth under the main hatchway, and slept on the boards. Having continued to live in this way for seven weeks, he found himself (if he can rightly use such language) seasoned and suited in constitution for the changes and scenes he had to undergo. His precaution had its uses, as perhaps nothing so much contributes to break down the soldier on service abroad as suddenly passing to extremes of climate, viz. from a temperate sky like ours to an opposite atmosphere, and perhaps from the heats of the line to chill countries like Canada.

April 20th. Our ship sailing at the rate of five miles an hour, a soldier whose name was Brooks, leaped off the forecastle into the ocean; the vessel in a moment made her way over him, and he arose at her stern. He immediately with all his might, swam from the ship.

The men who were upon the deck alarmed the captain and officers, who had just sat down to dinner; the ship was ordered to be put about, and the boat hoisted out, and manned, the unfortunate man was soon overtaken, and it was with difficulty that the sailors could force him into the boat. When he was brought back he was ordered between decks, and a centinel placed over him; the next morning he was in a high fever, and continued very bad the remainder of the voyage. The fear of punishment was the cause of this desperate action, as the day before he had stolen a shirt from one of his messmates knapsacks.[16]

30TH. The fleet sailing at the rate of six miles an hour: a serjeant had an altercation with his wife while they were sitting at breakfast, in consequence of which he got up in a rage, leaped overboard and was seen no more.[17]

MAY 3D. The wind strong at N. W. and running at the rate of seven miles an hour, one of the recruits stationed on the forecastle was so provoked by his comrades, that in a fit of rage he jumped over board, uttering at the same time dreadful curses upon them. He was swallowed up by the great deep in a moment!

14TH. Sailing over the banks of Newfoundland, we passed by several islands of ice, which came floating down from the river St. Lawrence. In sailing over the shoals or banks of Newfoundland, as usually happens, we seldom could behold the orb of the sun during the day. Here a thick hazy atmosphere generally hides the body of that glorious luminary which in most latitudes sheds animating light, and cheers the observer's eye. This heavy obscuration of the sky renders it very hazardous for a fleet to proceed as in other seas together. Sometimes total darkness like midnight covers the heav-

16. William Brooks was born in Stafford in 1751. "The Dying Declaration of James Buchanan, Ezra Ross and William Brooks," in Deborah Navas, *Murdered By His Wife: a History with Documentation of the Joshua Spooner Murder and Execution of His Wife, Bathsheba, Who Was Hanged in Worcester, Massachusetts, 2 July 1778* (Amherst: University of Massachusetts Press, 1999), 111.

17. A gap in the 9th Regiment's muster rolls makes it impossible to identify this sergeant.

ens, and at such times the unceasing firing of guns and beating of drums is necessary to enable the seamen to keep due distances, and prevent the ships from running foul of each other.

18TH. This morning we had a view of the mountains of Newfoundland, covered with snow; however, as we had been forty days at sea without seeing any land, this dreary island was very pleasant to our sight.

19TH. This day we entered the noble bay of St. Lawrence, between Cape de Retz, on the island of Newfoundland and Cape Breton, (our fleet all in sight,) and after doubling Cape Rosieres, we entered the river, which is in this place about ninety miles in breadth; here the sea was very boisterous.

20TH. Early this Morning the Island Anticosti presented itself to our sight, the current setting strongly in upon it, rendered our navigation extremely dangerous, especially as the island is lined with breakers. Our French pilot represented it as absolutely good for nothing; its coasts, however, are said to be well stored with fish.

21ST. This evening after passing the island of Anticosti, our navigation became more tolerable, but still the fleet used great precaution.

22D. The weather remarkably cold this day, but the wind fair, which soon brought us in sight of the Mounts Notre Dame and Lewis; here we saw for the first time, a number of neat French plantations. In the evening we sailed by Trinity Point, which we endeavoured to avoid with great care, and before dark we had a view of the Paps of Montani, so called from the appearance of the mountain, situated about two leagues from the shore.

23D. Our navigation was now very slow, the shores appeared uncomfortable, and uninhabited; in the evening we doubled a bay, called Tadoussac.

26TH. This day we sailed by the island of Caudres, which appeared to be very well inhabited and cultivated; churches, crucifixes, and images, were now to be seen almost every where: here the passage of the river is dangerous without a fair wind, in particular there is a whirlpool, which we carefully guarded against. Next appeared in our view, the Bay of St. Paul, where the plantations on the north shore begin; they consist of valuable woods of pine trees, among which are red pines, which are esteemed very beautiful. The village of St. Paul's is situated in a vale, and has a very romantic appearance from the river.

27TH. Early this morning we had a view of a very high promontory, which we were informed terminates a chain of mountains, that reach near five hundred leagues to the westward. This promontory is called Cape Torment. A number of islands now presented themselves to our view, among which is that of Orleans, which forms a most beautiful prospect, a clear open country, with villages, and churches innumerable, and being all whitewashed on the outside, gave them a neat, elegant appearance, from our ships. Here the water becomes fit to drink; for it is brackish at Cape Torment, though it is an hundred and ten leagues from the sea.

29TH. Our fleet now arrived at Quebec, which is the capital of the province of Canada, and an episcopal see.[18]

18. "See," the location of the cathedral in a diocese.

CHAPTER FOUR

[Campaign in Canada, 1776]

An attempt to surprise the British Troops at Three Rivers. Americans defeated. Retreat to St. John's. The British prepare a Fleet to cross Lake Champlain. Sails and engages the American Fleet, which is defeated. British Troops take possession of Crown Point. Return to Winter Quarters. A Soldier expires in quarters by excess rage.

IT IS NOW HIGH TIME to take notice of the military operations of the British forces to which I was attached in Canada. Colonel Arnold[1] raised the siege of Quebec and retreated with the greatest precipitation towards Three Rivers.

On the 29th June, 1776, having accomplished our voyage to Quebec, general Carleton[2] found himself at the head of twelve thousand regular troops, among whom were those of Brunswick.[3] With this force we set out for Three Rivers, where we expected that Arnold would have made a stand, but he had fled to Sorel, a place one hundred and fifty miles distant from Quebec, where he was at last met by the reinforcements, ordered by congress.

1. Benedict Arnold, at that time a colonel in the Continental army.
2. Sir Guy Carleton, commander in chief of the British army in Canada.
3. Regiments from the German principality of Brunswick. The German troops that served with the British army in American are popularly called "Hessians" even though many came from German states other than Hesse-Kassel and Hesse-Hanau.

In the mean time, our troops proceeded with all expedition from Quebec to Three Rivers, which place was appointed the general rendezvous of the army. In our passage up the river St. Lawrence, our eyes were entertained with beautiful landscapes, the banks being in many places very bold and steep, and shaded, with lofty trees, and in others crowded with villages, the air became so mild and temperate, that we thought ourselves transported into another climate. June 5th our regiment was ordered to land, and to press forward with all expedition. 6th, Arrived at Three Rivers.

June 8th. At three o'clock this morning our drums beat to arms, and we soon marched out of the village to meet our foe.

This being the first skirmish I ever was engaged in, it really appeared to me to be a very serious matter, especially when the bullets came whistling by our ears. In order to encourage the young soldiers amongst us, some of the veterans who had been well used to this kind of work, said, "there is no danger if you hear the sound of the bullet, which is fired against you, you are safe, and after the first charge all your fears will be done away." These remarks I found to be perfectly true many a time afterwards. The cannon from the ships in the river, and the field pieces on land, began now to roar; many of the unfortunate Americans were killed and wounded.

"Present we heard the battle's loud alarm,
"The hideous cannon with continued roar,
"Proclaims approaching death and wide spread harm:
"Confusion echoes from the martial shore."[4]

Surely war, whether offensive or defensive, is a picture of desolation!

This was a very bold enterprise indeed of the Americans to attack our troops. Two thousand of them crossed over from Sorel in fifty boats, landed at the Point du Lai, before day-light, with an intention to surprise us at Three Rivers. General Frazer,[5] who commanded

4. The source of this quote has not been identified.
5. Simon Frazer, lieutenant colonel of the 24th Regiment and brigadier general in America.

the British van,[6] was not to be taken by surprise. The Americans soon found that they were greatly mistaken in their intelligence concerning our position: when they discovered their mistake they were greatly alarmed, particularly when they found that brigadier general Nesbit,[7] who had landed the troops from the transports, had got behind them. After some time they gave up offensive measures, and retreated to the woods. Our troops still pushed forward in hopes of taking their boats and cutting off their retreat; two boats only were taken, the rest escaped. The number of the Americans killed and wounded were considerable; about two hundred surrendered, or were taken prisoners in the woods. Generals Thompson and Irwin, who commanded this party, with several other American officers, were among the prisoners: few of the British fell on this day.

9TH. Ordered on board our transports with all expedition; the wind springing up fair, the fleet sailed towards Sorel.

11TH. Our ship grounded on a sand bank, just in the middle of the river St. Lawrence; here we remained fast near two hours, and then drifted; we received no damage, and soon regained our station.

14TH. Landed at Sorel, here we heard that the Americans had retreated, only two hours before. All the fires in their encampment were burning.

15TH. Our troops began to march in three columns, under the command of general Burgoyne, who led the pursuit.

16TH. Continued our march day and night, expecting every hour to come up with them. However, in all their haste, they took care to set on fire their batteaux, ships, military stores, &c. It must be confessed that their distresses at this time were very great. A British army close on their rear, and threatening them with destruction; their men obliged to drag their loaded batteaux up the rapids by mere strength, often to their middle in water. They were likewise encumbered with great numbers labouring under that dreadful dis-

6. "Van," or vanguard, the lead corps in a military formation.

7. William Nesbit, lieutenant-colonel of the 47th Regiment and brigadier general in America.

ease, the small pox, which is so fatal in America. It was said that two regiments at one time had not a single man in health, another had only six, and a fourth only forty, and two more were nearly in the same condition.

While the Americans were retreating, they were daily annoyed by the remonstrances of the inhabitants of Canada, who had either joined or befriended them. Many of the Canadians had taken a decided part in their favor, rendered them essential services, and thereby incurred the heavy penalties annexed to the crime of supporting rebellion. These, though congress had assured them but a few months before, "that they would never abandon them to the fury of their common enemies," were, from the necessity of the case, left exposed to the resentment of their rulers. The retreating army recommended them to cast themselves on the mercy of that government, against which they had offended.*

18TH. Took possession of the redoubts[8] at St. John's, and found all the buildings in flames, all the craft and large boats the enemy could not drag up the rapids of Chamblee, with some provisions, were also burnt: twenty-two pieces of cannon were left behind, and several other marks appeared of great precipitation and fright, in the retreat of the enemy.

26TH. We heard that the Americans had retreated across Lake Champlain to Crown Point. We could not for want of boats urge our pursuit any farther.

SEPTEMBER 30TH. We have been very busy these three months past in constructing a fleet, in order to face the enemy on water. The spirit of our troops has risen in proportion to the difficulties which they had to encounter. A fleet is now prepared. The ship Inflexible,

*They did indeed receive mercy, for I never saw any of them either imprisoned or otherwise punished by our government, for their joining the Americans at this time; and I was in Canada for twelve months after this.

---

8. "Redoubts," earthen forts built as part of a system of fortifications.

mounting eighteen twelve-pounders[9] is ready to sail; three weeks ago her keel was laid. Two schooners, one of fourteen and another of twelve six-pounders. A flat bottom radeau,[10] carrying six twenty-four pounders, and six twelve-pounders, besides howitzers. A gondola, with seven nine-pounders. Twenty smaller vessels, with brass field pieces,[11] from nine to twenty-four pounders. A number of long boats. A great number of batteaux,[12] destined for the transportation of the army, have been in three months little less than created.

OCTOBER 1ST. Our little squadron was put under the command of Captain Pringle,[13] and is now ready to sail.

Upon the 11th, our squadron came up with the American fleet, commanded by Arnold; they were at anchor under the island Valicour,[14] and seemed a strong line, extending from the island to the west side of the continent. The wind was so unfavorable, that the ship Inflexible, and some other vessels of force, could not be brought to action.

Orders were now given to anchor, in a line as near as possible to the American fleet, that their retreat might be cut off. This was frustrated by the extreme obscurity of the night, and in the morning the American fleet had got a considerable distance from our ships up the lake.

13TH. Eleven sail of the Americans was seen making off to Crown Point, when after a chase of seven hours, captain Pringle, on board of the Maria, of fourteen six-pounders, having the armed vessels, Carleton and Inflexible, a small distance a-stern, came up with the enemy, the rest of the fleet almost out of sight. The action began at

9. Cannon were commonly referred to by the weight of their shot; a 12-pounder fired a 12-pound ball, etc.
10. "Radeau," a floating artillery battery.
11. "Field pieces," cannons on carriages with large wheels for use by the armies on campaign.
12. "Batteaux," long, flat-bottomed boats with pointed ends, commonly used on rivers.
13. Thomas Pringle, captain in the Royal Navy.
14. Valcour Island.

twelve o'clock, and lasted two hours. The Washington galley[15] struck[16] during the action, and some time after, Arnold in the Congress galley, and five gondolas,[17] ran on shore and blew up the vessels. In this perilous enterprize he paid attention to a point of honor. He did not quit his own galley till she was in flames, lest our sailors should board her, and strike her flag. The killed and wounded in our fleet did not amount to forty. General Carleton was on board the Maria during the action, and praised in the highest terms the conduct of the officers and men of the corps of artillery who served the gun boats, and who sustained for many hours the whole fire of the enemy's fleet, the rest of the vessels not being able to work up near enough to join effectually in the engagement.*

The Americans hearing of the defeat of their naval force, set fire to all the buildings and houses in and near Crown Point, and retired to Ticonderoga.

The result of this sea fight, though unfortunate for the Americans, raised the reputation of Arnold higher than ever; in addition to the fame of a brave soldier, he acquired that of an able naval officer. Waterburg,[18] the second in command, and brigadier general in the American army, was taken. Out of fifteen American armed vessels which engaged our fleet in the morning, three only escaped; the rest were taken, burnt and destroyed.

General Carleton landed at Crown Point, and took possession of the ground from which the Americans had retreated, and was there joined by our army. He sent out several reconnoitering parties,

*The matrosses who served in the gun-boats were drafts from the Irish Artillery in Chapelizod. [Editor: A matross was the lowest grade of private soldier in the artillery. The Royal Irish Regiment of Artillery had its principal barracks at Chapelizod, a suburb of Dublin. In early 1777, 70 men of the Royal Irish Artillery were drafted to serve in America. They were incorporated into the Royal Artillery serving in Burgoyne's army, and did not operate as a separate organization.]

15. "Galley," a vessel propelled by both oars and sails.
16. "Struck," surrendered by lowering its flag.
17. "Gondola," a type of flat-bottomed river boat.
18. David Waterbury, an American brigadier general.

and pushed forward a strong detachment on both sides of the lake, which approached near to Ticonderoga. Some of our vessels came within cannon shot of the American works at that place. But the strength of that garrison, and the season of the year restrained us from making any attempt, at that time, on Ticonderoga.

31st. Our army embarked on board of the batteaux, and on the 2d of November landed at St. John's, in Canada.

Such was the termination of the northern campaign in 1776. After the death of Montgomery, evacuations of posts, defeats, and retreats, had almost interruptedly[20] been the portion of the Americans.

The Winter Quarters of the British army was in the following order:

HEAD QUARTERS, QUEBEC.

Royal Artillery, commanded by General-Phillips[21]—General Hospital, Montreal.

Van Brigade, commanded by gen. Frazer, Grenadiers, light Infantry and 24th regiment—At Le Prairie, Longeuil, &c. extending on the south side of the river St. Lawrence to St. Curs.

First Brigade commanded by brigadier general Powel.[22]

9th regiment—Isle Jesus.

47th do.[23]—St. Luce, Recollet, St. Geneviere and St. Lawrent.*

53d—Chamblee.

Second Brigade, commanded by brigadier general Hamilton.[24]

20th regiment—Isle au Noix.

21st do—St. John's.

*Lieutenant colonel Nesbit died about this time, at Quebec, he was a brave, humane officer, and greatly beloved by the brigade which he commanded.

---

20. Lamb clearly means "uninterruptedly."
21. William Phillips, major general commanding the artillery in Canada and on Burgoyne's campaign.
22. Henry Watson Powell, lieutenant-colonel of the 53rd Regiment.
23. "do.", that is, ditto.
24. James Hamilton, lieutenant-colonel of the 21st Regiment.

34th do—Quebec.

62d do—Point Levy, opposite to Quebec.

German troops commanded by generals Reidesel[25] and Specht,[26] were quartered from Bertheier to Three Rivers, and forty miles below Three Rivers, on the road to Quebec.

Maclean's Royal Highlanders, emigrants, quartered at Chinage Bonne, and River du China.

Sir John Johnson's regiment, called the New Yorker's, quartered at Lachine, La Point Clare, and St. Ann.

8th regiment—Upper Posts, Niagara, Detroit, &c.

During our stay in Canada the army had sufficient time for providing to meet the enemy, and although in thus preparing the troops were much occupied in acquiring whatever efficiency training and exercise could produce, yet comparatively with actual engagements such a season was a time of inactivity. In cantonments the greatest care of the commander is wanted to keep regiments well regulated and in order, as numbers of the soldiery will take occasion to indulge in disorderly habits, and so become worse in all respects. Means should be used therefore to keep the men regularly and usefully employed, so as to inspire them, as much as can be, with good impressions of duty and even moral propriety. It may be thought, that to attempt mental reformation among an army would be vain, but something in this way might be effected, and even salutary amendments produced which might excite surprise. At all events strict precautionary measures should never be remitted, as from the remissness of command and lax discipline, accidents of misbehaviour, riot, and outrage cannot fail to happen. A case in some way illustrative of this argument occurred while we were cantoned in Canada. A soldier notorious for wickedness and boisterous temper, quarrelling with one of the men, and, no doubt, knowing he could

25. Baron Friedrich von Riedesel, commander of the German contingent of the British army in Canada.

26. Johann Friedrich Specht, colonel of the Regiment Specht.

not with impunity gratify his rage, expired in excess of anger. He was remarkable for blasphemous swearing and the worst conduct, and his awful manner of dying made a solemn impression on the minds of the soldiers, when they considered his profane life and sudden decease.

Canadians appear somewhat peculiar in religious observance, particularly in their erecting large crosses and representations of saints upon the highway. The procession of Holy Thursday, which they entitle *La fete Dieu*, cannot but engage the attention of travellers. On the day previous to one of these processions we were noticed of it, and his Majesty (in consequence of indecorous behaviour, and bad accidents happening on the like religious occasions) having made some time before a proclamation, that proper respect should be observed by the military on such celebrations, General Philips issued orders in pursuance of it. The General's order required that, "non-commissioned officers be particular in informing the men that, when the host should go by they were to front it, and behave in a decent and respectable manner, to pull off their hats and remain in that situation until the host should pass." The order added, that any complaint made, to the General of misbehaviour, if proved, should be punished with the utmost severity. This is a case in point to shew that our gracious Sovereign always provided for the religious toleration and civil liberty of his subjects, and that officers commanding were strictly attentive to give his Majesty's paternal desires their due effect.

CHAPTER FIVE

[Burgoyne's Campaign]

Northern Army opens the Campaign. Crosses Lake Champlain. Ticonderoga taken. Fort Ann evacuated by the Americans. British Troops move forward to Fort Edward and Fort Miller. Germans are defeated at Bennington. British Army crosses Hudson's River. Desperate Attacks made on the British Army. Are obliged to retreat. Surrenders at Saratoga.

IN THE BEGINNING OF JUNE, 1777, the northern army, which consisted of four thousand British troops, and three thousand Germans, marched from their winter quarters, in the different parts of Canada, and encamped on the western side of Lake Champlain. Here they were joined by some Canadians, and the army was put under the command of general Burgoyne. The soldiers were in a high state of discipline, and had been kept in their winter quarters with the greatest care, in order to prepare them for this expedition.

The British army proceeded up Lake Champlain, in batteaux, in the greatest order and regularity, and landed at the river Boquet, near Crown Point. Here a body of Indians joined it. In crossing the lakes the Indians in their canoes, containing from twenty to thirty men each, headed our troops as they sailed in brigade. One brigade regularly followed the other, proceeding from about seventeen to twenty miles a day. The order of progress was so regulated that the next following brigade occupied at night the encampment which the immediately preceding one left in the morning. After the Indians, the advanced corps sailed in regular line with the Royal George and Inflexible war ships coming after, towing large booms, which were used to be thrown across two points of land. Then came the brigs and sloops, and after them the first brigade, having the pinnaces of Generals Burgoyne, Philips, and Reidesel, in rear of them. Next followed the second brigade, and last the German brigade, whose rear was brought up by the *suttlers*[1] *and followers* of the army.

Although the waters of the Champlain are frequently much agitated, our army in passing found it serene and tranquil. At one time it afforded a delightful appearance. Undisturbed by a breeze its clear, chrystal surface became like an indefinitively extended mirror, reflecting the heavens, and green umbrage of the trees which bordered the islands of the lake, while at the same time the entire army moved majestically along in perfect order. It looked like some stupendous fairy scene of a dream, which the waking fancy can scarcely conceive. Picture to yourself a sheet of fine water, where the horizon interposed between the farther shore, with an army of men embarked upon it, islands covered with tall trees, and the sky calm and smiling. One would be tempted to forget that the element on which he sailed was often subject to storms and shipwreck, and that while its aspect was so inviting it became a swift medium to carry him to fields of carnage and desolation. Yet such was in reality the case. Lake Champlain is much exposed to gales which blow in squalls from the high mountainous lands on the north. One of these squalls took our army in sailing, but without any damage, except to a small brig which was laid on her side, and saved by cutting away her masts. During the gale of wind we encountered, it was feared the Indians must have perished, but, contrary to our apprehensions, their canoes rode the storm without injury.

1. "Sutlers," merchants licensed by the army to sell liquor and sometimes food and other goods to soldiers.

While we passed Lake Chaplain, it happened to be the season when wild pigeons migrate in flocks over the lakes to Canada, and our meeting with these airy voyagers afforded us much amusement. The most of them were decorated with beautiful plumage, and their flight must be from far, as several of them were much wearied, with difficulty gaining the trees to rest on, and dropping even in the water. On these occasions the soldiers, as the vessels sailed along the islands, struck them down, and picked them up as they fell.

In passing the lakes we frequently encamped, and at each encampment were obliged to clear off the underwood, and cut away the small trees from about us. On such occasions we were constantly assailed by venemous swarms of musquitoes, that could not be kept from attacking us but by the smoke and flame of large fires, which we always were obliged to kindle for banishing this noxious vermin.

On the 30th of June, the British advanced to Crown Point, about twelve miles from Ticonderoga. In the evening the following orders were given: "The army embarks to-morrow, to approach the enemy. The services required on this expedition are critical and conspicuous. During our progress occasions may occur, in which, nor difficulty, nor labour, nor life, are to be regarded. This army must not retreat." From Crown Point they proceeded to invest Ticonderoga. On their approach to it they advanced on both sides of the lake, while the naval force kept in the centre. Within a few days they had surrounded three fourths of the American works at Ticonderoga, and Mount Independence, and had also advanced a work on Sugar Hill, the top of which overlooked and effectually commanded the whole works. The Americans vainly imagining that the difficulty of the ascent would be sufficient to prevent the British troops from taking possession of it. On the approach of the first division of the army, the Americans abandoned and set fire to their out works, and so expeditious were the advances, that by the 5th of July, every post was secured which was judged necessary for investing it compleatly. A road was soon after made to the summit of that eminence, which the Americans had with such confidence supposed could not be ascended; and so much were they disheartened, that they instantly abandoned the fort entirely, taking the road to Skeensborough, a place to the south of Lake George, while their baggage, with what artillery and military stores they could carry off, were sent to the same place by water. But the British generals were determined not to let them pass so easy; both were pursued and overtaken; their armed vessels consisted only of five galleys, two of which were taken and three blown up, on which they set fire to their boats and fortifications at Skeensborough. On this occasion the Americans lost two hundred boats, one hundred and thirty pieces of cannon, with all their provisions and baggage.

After the enemy retreated we marched down to the works, and were obliged to halt at the bridge of communication which had been broken down. In passing the bridge and possessing ourselves of the works we found four men lying intoxicated with drinking, who had been left to fire the guns of a large battery on our approach. Had the men obeyed the commands they received, we must have suffered great injury, but they were allured by the opportunity of a cask of Madeira to forget their instructions, and drown their cares in wine. It appeared evident that they were left for the purpose alluded to, as matches were found lighted, the ground was strewed with powder, and the heads of some powder casks were knocked off in order, no doubt, to injure our men in their gaining the works. An Indian had like to do some mischief from his curiosity—holding a lighted match near one of the guns; it exploded, but being elevated, it discharged without harm.

At the break of day, July the 6th, the American land forces, under colonel Francis, were eagerly pursued by brigadier general Frazer, at the head of his brigade, consisting of the grenadiers and light infantry, and overtook him at Hibbertown.[2] The grenadiers were or-

2. The battle at Hubbardton, Vermont, was fought on 7 July 1777. Colonel Ebenezer Francis commanded the 11th Massachusetts Regiment, a portion of the American force in the battle.

dered to form and prevent him in the road to Castletown. Being turned in this direction, the enemy attempted to proceed to Pittsford, by a steep mountainous road. In this attempt they were thrown into much confusion by means of our grenadiers, who climbed a very steep ascent to stop their march. In climbing this high ground, which looked inaccessible, the men encountered great fatigue and danger, being obliged to sling their firelocks to their sides,[3] and sometimes ascend by laying hold of the branches of trees. After gaining the summit of this elevated ground, the grenadiers had hard fighting before they prevailed against the Americans, who were greatly superior in numbers, and commanded by a brave officer, Colonel Francis, who fell in the fight. They made (considering the opposition of raw and undisciplined troops to veteran soldiers) a brave defence. As they were greatly superior to the British in numbers, they had almost overpowered general Frazer, when general Reidesel, with a large body of Germans, came to his assistance; the Americans were then overpowered in their turn, their commander and above two hundred men killed, and as many taken prisoners. {It is not unworthy to observe that the German troops prepared for the conflict as they approached the field of battle by singing Psalms, and that the effect of their onset and charge, followed by an incessant fire on their part, gave a sudden and signal decision to the severe action of the day.} They were about 2000 in number, while the British amounted but to 850, who maintained the conflict during two hours previous to the coming up of the Germans, whose accession of force fortunately decided a hard fought affair. The loss of the British was very inconsiderable; major Grant of the 24th regiment, a brave officer, fell on that day.[4] Lord Balcarras, who command the light infantry, had his coat and trowsers pierced with about thirty balls, and escaped with a slight wound, while in the

3. The firelock had a leather sling which allowed it to be hung over the soldier's shoulder.
4. Robert Grant, major in the 24th Regiment of Foot.

same battle Lieut. Haggit, in the opening attack, received a mortal wound in both eyes by a ball, and Lieut. Douglass of the 29th, while some of the men were taking him wounded from the field, was killed with a ball, which took him in the heart.[5]

The nature of hostilities on the American continent acquired a sort of implacable ardour and revenge, which happily are a good deal unknown the prosecution of war in general. This remark is justified by the fate of Captain Shrimpton, of the 62d regiment, after the battle just mentioned.[6] Some of our officers stood examining papers taken from the pocket of Colonel Francis on the field. As the Captain held the papers he leaped and exclaimed that he was badly wounded. The officers heard the whizzing of the ball, and saw the smoke of the fire, but failed to find the man who aimed with such effect, and escaped without seizure, or even being seen.

In fighting in the woods the battalion manœuvring and excellency of exercise were found of little value.[7] To prime, load, fire and charge with the bayonet expeditiously were the chief points worthy of attention. It was our custom after loading and priming, instead of ramming down cartridge, to strike the breech of the firelock to the ground, and bring it to the present and fire.[8] In this usage much care was necessary, lest the cartridge might remain undischarged, as sometimes happened, when, from the confusion of the moment of action, the end of the cartridge being unbitten it might not catch fire from the burnt priming. In this way several cartridges have been discovered together in the piece unexploded, which, in the bursting of his firelock from an overcharge, could not fail to be very perilous

5. Alexander Lindsay, Earl of Balcarras, at this time major of the 53rd Regiment of Foot, became the lieutenant-colonel of the 24th Regiment on October 8, 1777. James Haggart, a lieutenant in the Marines serving as a lieutenant in the grenadier company of the 34th Regiment. James Douglas, a lieutenant in the 29th Regiment.
6. John Shrimpton, captain commanding the grenadier company of the 62nd Regiment.
7. That is, the close order movements of companies and entire regiments, which were widely practiced during peacetime for warfare in Europe.
8. "Present," the aiming position in the British manual of arms.

and sometimes destructive to the soldier himself, and even some of those around him.[9]

Such was the rapid torrent of success, which in this period of the campaign, swept away all opposition before the British army. The officers and men, were highly elated with their good fortune. They considered their toils to be nearly at an end; Albany to be within their grasp, and the adjacent provinces reduced to a certainty. The terror which the loss of Ticonderoga spread throughout the New England States was great; but nevertheless, no disposition to purchase safety by submission appeared in any quarter. The army after these successes continued some time in Skeensborough, waiting for their tents, baggage, and provisions. In the mean time, general Burgoyne detached the 9th regiment, commanded by lieutenant colonel Hill, to Fort Ann, a place of some strength, in order to intercept such of the enemy as should attempt to retreat towards that Fort.[10] We had not proceeded many miles through the woods, before we overtook some boats laden with baggage, women, and invalids belonging to the Americans, rowing up wood creek in order to escape Fort Ann. The woods being very thick hid the creek from our view and the whole Regiment was ordered to fire a volley near the place where the noise of the oars were heard; the boats stopped immediately. Two ladies were wounded one of them through her breasts and brought on shore; being the assistant surgeon I dressed their wounds, gave them some refreshment, left then in a hut and proceeded with my regiment. When the regiment returned a few days afterwards the Colonel took them under his protection. One of

9. Here Lamb explains that the close order movements taught in training were of little use in the American war. Ammunition carried by soldiers was in the form of cartridges, paper tubes filled with a musket ball and a measured charge of gunpowder. To load the firelock, the soldier used his teeth to tear one end off of the cartridge, poured a small amount of powder into the priming pan on the side of the firelock, and put the remaining powder and the ball into the barrel. Normally the ball was rammed down with a ramrod, but Lamb indicates that, to save time, soldiers forced the powder and ball down the barrel by banging the butt of the firelock on the ground.

10. John Hill, lieutenant-colonel of the 9th Regiment of Foot.

As the 9th Regiment of Foot advanced through wilderness towards Fort Anne in July 1777, they fired blindly upon boats carrying American invalid soldiers and women, wounding two of the latter. Lamb described the event in detail in his commonplace book, and included this illustration, but glossed over it in his published books. Methodist Historical Society of Ireland.

these ladies was the innocent cause of my running the gauntlet in New England when I was a prisoner there 12 months afterwards.[11] We then proceeded on our march, till we came within a quarter of a mile of Fort Ann, which was at that time garrisoned by a strong party of the enemy; we halted and lay upon our arms all night.

Early next morning, 9th July, an American soldier came from the fort; he said that he had deserted, though it was afterwards discovered that he was a spy; he stated that there were one thousand men in the fort, and that they were in the greatest consternation, under an apprehension of the British attacking and storming them; upon this intelligence colonel Hill dispatched a message to general Bur-

11. This passage, from "We had not proceeded many miles," is from the commonplace book.

goyne stating his situation, and how far he had advanced, which was eight or ten miles from the main army.

Not many minutes after this message was sent off, the pretended deserter disappeared; he had viewed the situation and seen the strength of the British, which did not amount to above one hundred and ninety men including officers. It was soon found that he made a faithful report to his friends, for in less than half an hour they came out of the fort with great fury. The British outline of centries received them with the greatest bravery and steadiness, and obliged them to retreat; they then formed again, and came on with redoubled violence. The officers could be heard encouraging them on to the attack, though their numbers could not be seen, the woods being so thick, but it was soon found that they not only out flanked but were endeavoring to surround the British; in order to prevent this they were obliged to change their ground, and retire up a high hill, which was in their rear; in performing this manœuvre several of the men were killed and wounded.[12] When the troops arrived at the summit of the hill they formed in Indian file,[13] and kept up a well directed fire till all the ammunition was expended; the enemy observing that the firing ceased, was encouraged to press forward with redoubled vigour and endeavoured to surround them in order to cut off all retreat. Just at this critical moment a war hoop was heard, which resounded through the wood; this sound, which was so obnoxious at that time to the Americans, threw them into the utmost consternation.[14]

The war hoop was sounded by captain Money, deputy quarter master general;[15] he had been detached by general Burgoyne early

12. That is, the British moved to a position on the hill in order to avoid being surrounded by the Americans.

13. "Indian file," a single file line; the British army more commonly used double- or triple-files.

14. "War hoop," the whooping noise used by the Indians when going into battle.

15. John Money, a captain in the 9th Regiment of Foot. Some sources confuse him an officer of the same name in the 63rd Regiment who was an aide de camp to General Cornwallis later in the war.

in the morning from Skeensborough, with a party of Indians, in order to join this detachment when they came within four miles of Fort Ann, they heard the firing; Captain Money ordered them to advance as fast as possible to assist, but they refused to obey him, and either stood still or advanced very slow. Being anxious to join the party at all events, he ran forward by himself with all his might, and came to the bottom of the hill where, just as all the ammunition was expended, he gave the war hoop.

In this affair the British had three officers and nineteen men killed and wounded.

Captain Montgomery, son to Sir W. Montgomery, bart. of Dublin, was wounded in the leg and taken prisoner, with the surgeon who was dressing his wound, just before we retired up the hill.[16] I very narrowly escaped myself from being taken prisoner at that time, as I was just in the act of assisting the surgeon in dressing the captain's wound, when the enemy came pouring down upon us like a mighty torrent, in consequence whereof I was the last man that ascended the hill. I had not been there five minutes when lieutenant Westrop, who was by my side was shot through the heart;[17] a few minutes after a man, a short distance upon my left, received a ball in his forehead, which took off the roof of his scull! he reeled round, turned up his eyes, muttered some words, and fell dead at my feet! After the Americans had retreated, we formed on the hill. It was a distressing sight to see the wounded men bleeding on the ground, and what made it more so the rain came pouring down like a deluge upon us; and still to add to the distress of the sufferers, there was nothing to dress their wounds, as the small medicine box which was filled with salve, was left behind with surgeon Shelly and captain Montgomery at the time of our movement up the hill. The poor fellows earnestly entreated me to tie up their wounds. Immediately I took off my shirt, tore it up, and with the help of a soldier's

16. William Stone Montgomery, a captain in the 9th Regiment of Foot.

17. Richard Westropp, a lieutenant in the 9th Regiment of Foot.

wife, (the only woman that was with us, and who kept close by her husband's side during the engagement,) made some bandages, stopped the bleeding of their wounds, and conveyed them in blankets to a small hut about two miles in our rear. In the mean time, general Burgoyne having heard of our critical situation, moved forward at the head of a strong detachment, in order to support us; but the Americans had set fire to Fort Ann, and fled with great precipitation, before his arrival. Our regiment marched back to Skeensborough, leaving me behind to attend the wounded, with a small guard for our protection. I was directed, that in case I should be either surrounded or overpowered by the Americans, to deliver a letter, which general Burgoyne gave me, to their commanding officer. Here I remained seven days with the wounded men, expecting every moment to be taken prisoner; but, although we heard the enemy cutting down trees every night during our stay, in order to block up the passages of the road and river, yet we were never molested. Every necessary which we wanted was sent us from the camp at Skeensborough, and all the wounded men (except three who died) were nearly fit for duty when we arrived at head quarters.

The British were now obliged to suspend all operations for some time, and wait at Skeensborough for the arrival of provisions and tents; but they employed this interval clearing a passage for the troops, to proceed against the enemy. This was attended with incredible toil. The Americans, now under the direction of general Schuyler,[18] were constantly employed in cutting down large trees on both sides of every road, which was in the line of march. The face of the country was likewise so broken with creeks and marshes, that there were no less than forty bridges to construct, one of which was over a morass two miles in extent. The difficulties of the march through this wilderness were encountered and overcome by the army with a spirit and alacrity which could not be exceeded; and on the 20th of July, it encamped at Fort Edward. General Schuyler now

18. Philip Schuyler, an American major general.

retreated to Saratoga, and immediately issued a proclamation warning the Americans that they would be dealt with as traitors, if they joined the British army, and requiring them, with their arms, to repair to the American standard.[19] At the same time numerous parties were employed in desolating the country, felling trees, and throwing every obstruction in the way of the army. Indeed at first an universal panic intimidated the inhabitants, but they soon recovered from its operation.

From the encampment of Fort Edward, the expedition to Bennington was undertaken, and maintained chiefly by the Germans; although the British thought that they themselves ought to have been employed chiefly in it. This issue of this operation in its failure was differently accounted for; but the principal cause seemed to be owing to the delay of marching to the place. The expedition set out at eight o'clock in the forenoon, and did not arrive there, although but twenty-two miles, until four o'clock in the afternoon of the next day![20]

The soldier's labour began at this period to become severe in an extraordinary measure. In marching through a difficult country, he was obliged to bear a burden which none except the old Roman veteran ever bore. He carried a knapsack, blanket, haversack containing four day's provisions, a canteen for water, and a proportion of his tent furniture, which, superadded to his accoutrements, arms and sixty rounds of ammunition, made a great load and large luggage, weighing about sixty pounds.[21] The German grenadiers, from their cumbrous armour,[22] long clothing and big canteen, holding a gallon,

19. "repair to the American standard," join the American army.

20. The expedition to Bennington, Vermont, culminated in a battle and defeat on August 16, 1777.

21. This heavy load was born by British soldiers only in situations when they were on campaign and without baggage wagons or batteaux. British soldiers most often marched only with blankets and provisions, leaving knapsacks, tents and other equipment in wagons. Notice that Lamb mentioned the army stopping after taking Ticonderoga to wait for their tents, whereas now he says the soldiers were carrying their tents.

22. Presumably a reference to the tall miter caps with brass front plates worn by the German grenadiers; they did not wear armor per se.

were much worse circumstanced than our men for the wearisome marches we made.

As the royal troops advanced towards the enemy along the side of Hudson's river, they found the country covered with thick woods, and the bridges broken down every quarter of a mile; these they were obliged to repair. Every obstacle to impede their march was thrown in their way, and they soon discovered that the Americans were determined to dispute every inch of the ground with them.

During our continuance at Fort Miller,[23] the writer of this memoir was selected by his officers to return alone to Ticonderoga, for the purpose of taking back some of our baggage which had been left there. Going unaccompanied on such a solitary route was dreary and dangerous; but yet the selection of one from numbers, seemed to render the man chosen on the occasion, a depositary of peculiar confidence. He therefore undertook the duty imposed, not only without repining, but with alacrity. A small detachment if sent, could not pass unnoticed or safe by such a route through the woods, a distance of twenty miles; and a sufficient force could not be spared on the occasion. The sending of a single soldier appeared therefore the most adviseable plan; and it was ordered by General Burgoyne, that he should, after arriving at Ticonderoga, follow the royal army with the baggage, escorted by the recruits,[24] and as many of the convalescents remaining at that post as could march with it. Pursuant to this arrangement, he prepared himself, taking twenty rounds of ball cartridge, and some provisions. About noon he set out, and at four in the afternoon reached our former encampment, Fort Edward, where he stopped a while to refresh. From thence he proceeded with as much expedition as he could make to Fort Henry, on Lake George. About eleven o'clock at night, becoming very weary, he laid him down to sleep a little in a thick part of a wood.

23. Fort Miller on the west shore of the Hudson River, not far from Fort Edward.

24. British recruits that arrived in Quebec after Burgoyne's expedition had departed made their way to Ticonderoga in late August.

Although the day was hot, the night dews soon awakened him, shivering with cold; having rested but about two hours, and then resuming his march for four or five miles, he saw a light on his left, and directed his course toward it. Having gained the place, he was saluted by a man at the door of his house, who informed him that a soldier's wife had been just taken in from the woods, where she was found by one of his family, in the pains of child-birth. Being admitted into this hospitable dwelling, the owner of which was one of the Society of Friends, or people called Quakers, he recognized the wife of a serjeant of his own company. The woman was delivered of a fine girl soon after; and having requested her friendly host to allow her to stop until his return from Ticonderoga, at which time he would be able to take her to the army in one of the waggons, he set out on his lonely route again. Previous to his leaving her, she informed him that she had determined to brave the dangers of the woods, in order to come up with her husband;[25] that she crossed Lake George, and was seized with the sickness of labour in the forest, where she must have perished, had she not been providentially discovered by the kind-hearted people under whose roof she then was. It is worthy of remark, that the author, not long since in this city,[26] with great pleasure, saw the female, who was born as he before related, in the wilderness, near Lake George. She had been married to a man serving in the band of a militia regiment, and the meeting with her, revived in his mind lively emotions of distressful and difficult scenes, which although long passed, can never be forgotten by him. At Fort George he was provided with a boat to take him across the Lake to Ticonderoga.

The author having arrived and completed his business at Ticonderoga, he accompanied the baggage over Lake George, attended by a number of seamen sent to work the *batteaux* on the Hudson

25. When the expedition marched from Canada, only three women per company were allowed on the march. On this and other campaigns, some wives made their own way to join their husbands even though prohibited from actually marching with the army.
26. That is, in Dublin.

river. On his returning he called with the good Quaker who lodged the sick wife of his fellow soldier, but to his astonishment was told that, on the morrow after he left her there in child-birth, she set out to meet her husband against the wishes and repeated entreaties of the whole family, who were anxious to detain her until his return. She could not be persuaded to stop, but set out on foot with her new-born infant, and arrived safe with her husband, whom she followed with such fond solicitude. She thus gave an instance of the strength of female attachment and fortitude, which shews that the exertions of the sex are often calculated to call forth our cordial admiration. In a short time the author had the gratification of conducting the stores and baggage for which he was dispatched, in safety to the army, and to receive the thanks of his officers, for the manner in which he executed the orders confided to him.

By this conveyance the forces obtained a month's provisions, and a bridge of boats being constructed upon the Hudson, on the 13th and 14th September, 1777, the royal army crossed it, and encamped on Saratoga plain. Here the country looked like a desert—no inhabitant remained to be seen. On the 15th the forces moved forward to an encampment, in a place called Devaco.[27] Halting till the 17th, our troops renewed their march, rebuilding several bridges which had been broken, and encamped on a ground of considerable advantage, distant about four miles from Still Water, where the enemy stood strongly posted. On the 18th he appeared in force to obstruct the men employed in repairing the bridges, who suffered some losses. It was suspected that he designed to draw our army to action, where the artillery could not engage. At this encampment several of our men having proceeded into a field of potatoes, were surprised by a party of the enemy that killed about thirty of them. They might without difficulty be surrounded and taken prisoners, but the Americans could not resist the opportunity of shedding blood. Such a spirit of revenge, however, had better, for the sake of

27. Dovecote, also known as Dovegat or Dovegate, is today called Coveville, New York.

humanity been controuled, because it only tended to excite destructive retaliation on the side of our army. But such ardent asperity sharpened a conflict which arose in the unfortunate falling out of friends, and made it more sanguinary than the hostilities of states that cherish no kindred relations.

September 19th. The royal army halted within two miles of the enemy's encampment, and formed for battle. The signal guns, which had been previously settled to give notice that all was ready, now fired, and the troops advanced in the greatest order and regularity. And in about an hour the advanced party, consisting of the picquets[28] of the centre column, commanded by Major Forbes,[29] fell in with a considerable body posted in houses and behind fences, which they attacked, and after much firing, nearly drove in the body of the Americans, but the woods were filled with men which annoyed our picquets, who must have greatly suffered had they not been fortunately supported by two companies of the 24th, and a piece of artillery, which obliged the enemy to retreat.

In the mean time the Americans came out of their entrenchments in great force, and moved forward to meet the British army. Their line extended upwards of two miles, while they were supported by several strong columns. The scouts and flankers of both armies were soon in contact, and the firing began a little after mid-day.

The Americans being incapable from the nature of the country, of perceiving the different combinations of the march* , advanced a strong column, with a view of turning the British line upon the right;[30] here they met the grenadiers and light infantry, who gave them a tremendous fire. Finding that it was impossible to penetrate

*As the country is thickly covered with woods, movements may be effected without a possibility of being discovered.

---

28. "Picquets," soldiers arranged in a very loose, open formation as an advanced guard.
29. Gordon Forbes, major in the 9th Regiment of Foot.
30. That is, the Americans did not realize that they were facing the center column of the three British columns; in attempting to outflank the center column, they ran into the right column.

the line at this point, they immediately countermarched and directed their principal effort to the centre. Here the conflict was dreadful; for four hours a constant blaze of fire was kept up, and both armies seemed to be determined on death or victory.

"Here mingling hands, but not with friendly gripe,
Join in the fight; and breasts in close embrace,
But mortal as the iron arms of death.
Here words austere, of perilous command,
And valour swift t'obey; bold feats of arms
Dreadful to see, and glorious to relate."[31]

Men, and particularly officers, dropped every moment on each side. Several of the Americans placed themselves in high trees, and as often as they could distinguish a British officer's uniform, took him off by deliberately aiming at his person. Reinforcements successively arrived and strengthened the American line. The 20th, 21st, and 62d regiments greatly distinguished themselves. The stress of the action lay chiefly on these regiments, which stood the repeated attacks of three times their number for four hours.

"Not noise, nor number, nor the brawny limb,
Nor high built size prevails: 'Tis courage fights,
'Tis courage conquers."[32]

Most of the other corps of the army bore a good share in this desperate conflict. The 24th regiment, with the grenadiers, and part of the light infantry, were for some time brought into action, and charged with their usual spirit and bravery. Breyman's riflemen likewise did good service.[33]

Major General Phillips, upon hearing the firing, made his way through a difficult part of the wood to the scene of action, and

31. From Isaac Watts, *The celebrated Victory of the Poles over Osman, the Turkish Emperor, in the Dacian Battle*, 1706.
32. From Watts, *The celebrated Victory*, 1706.
33. Heinrich Christoph Breymann, lieutenant-colonel commanding the German advanced corps in Burgoyne's army.

brought up with him major Williams and four pieces of artillery;[34] this reinforcement animated our troops in the centre, which at that moment were critically pressed by a great superiority of fire, and to which the major general led up the 20th regiment at the utmost personal hazard. Major general Reidesel then brought forward part of the left wing, and arrived in time to charge the enemy with regularity and bravery.

Few actions have been characterized by more obstinacy in attack or defence; the British troops repeatedly tried their bayonet with their usual success. A little before night set in, the enemy gave way on all sides, but the darkness saved him from our pursuit.[35] During the night we rested on our arms, and next day took a position within cannon-shot of the enemy's lines.

It was supposed that during this engagement near fifteen hundred men were killed and wounded in both armies. The British had to lament more than three hundred brave officers and men, who were killed and wounded on that day! In this fight our forces had to encounter a variety of great difficulties. The local situation favoured our adversaries, who trebled us in numbers. Although we repulsed them with loss, we ourselves were much weakened, so that we could not follow the advantages of the victory obtained. We kept the field, and the possession of it was the utmost point gained.

20TH. The army moved forward, and took post nearly within cannon shot of the American's fortified camp. Here the English strengthened their camp by cutting down large trees, which served for breast works. The ground afforded a scene truly distressing—the bodies of the slain, thrown together into one receptacle, were scarcely covered with the clay, and the only tribute of respect to fallen officers was, to bury them by themselves, without throwing them in the common grave. In this battle an unusual number of of-

34. Griffith Williams, captain in the Royal Artillery with the staff position of Extra Major of Brigade.
35. This was the Battle of Freeman's Farm, also called the First Battle of Saratoga.

ficers fell, as our army abounded with young men of respectability at this time, who, after several years of general peace anterior to the American revolution, were attracted to take the profession of arms. Three subalterns of the 20th regiment on this occasion, the oldest of whom did not exceed the age of seventeen years, were buried together.[36]

Although the duty of interring the slain be thus a sad business to the party that does it, the picking up the badly wounded, who are found weltering in their blood, and agonized for many hours without the possibility of receiving surgical and medical aid, imposes a task of heartfelt trouble on the men that execute it. So it was on the next day after the fight described. Some of our soldiers were discovered alive, who had rather stay as they were, than be pained by a removal from the field. Some were insensible, benumbed with the night dews, and weakened with loss of blood, while others seemed to have arrived at the extreme point of suffering, when a desirable separation of partnership between the soul and the body was about to deliver them from a troublesome state.

OCTOBER 3D. This day the rations were diminished. The army saw the necessity of this measure. Not a complaint or murmur was heard throughout the British camp.

7TH. Matters were drawing at this time to a crisis—Our picquets and advanced parties were almost continually firing and skirmishing, so much so that the officers and men refreshed and slept while exposed to the enemy's fire. All rested in their cloaths, and the Field-officers[37] were always patroling. We could distinctly hear the Americans felling and cutting trees; and they had a piece of ordnance which they used to fire as a morning gun, so near us, that the wadding from it sometimes struck against our works.[38] General

36. "Subalterns," officers below the rank of captain.

37. "Field officers," regimental officers above the rank of captain.

38. "Wadding," cloth or paper inserted into a cannon barrel after the powder and ball, to seal any gaps between the charge and the barrel. A morning gun was fired as a time signal using only powder and wadding.

Corporal of the 9th Regiment of Foot, as he may have looked on Burgoyne's campaign in 1777. His coat has been shortened, and his breeches and gaiters have been replaced by canvas trousers fitted to his legs and ankles. His felt hat is reconfigured into a cap with a cast metal numeral on the front. He wears his waistbelt over his shoulder, along with a canvas haversack filled with three days' rations of cooked meat and bread, plus fruits and vegetables he foraged locally. The top of his tin canteen is just visible behind the haversack, suspended from his shoulder by a cord. He does not wear his knapsack, which is still carried on boats or baggage carts at this stage of the campaign. A white epaulet on his right shoulder indicates his rank. Illustration by Eric Schnitzer.

Burgoyne was now most unfavourably posted, and a retreat, if possible, was highly expedient. In this idea he sent out a detachment of 1500 men, with two twelve-pounders about noon, to perceive, if it were practicable, to force a passage to Albany, by dislodging the enemy, and covering the forage of the army, which became scarce. On this important affair he was accompanied by Generals Philips, Reidesel, and Frazer.

As they advanced they were checked by a very sudden and rapid attack of the enemy on the left; there major Ackland was posted with the British grenadiers, who sustained the attack with great resolution and firmness.[39] The Americans extended their attack along the whole front of the German troops, who were posted on the right of the grenadiers, and they also marched a large body round their flanks, in order to cut off their retreat. To oppose this bold enterprize the British light infantry, with a part of the 24th regiment, were directed to form a second line, and to secure the return of the troops into camp. In the mean time, the Americans pushed forward a fresh and a strong reinforcement to renew the action upon the left; where the troops, overpowered by so great a superiority, gave way, but the light infantry and 24th regiment, by a rapid movement, came to give succour, and saved the line from being carried; in doing which, brigadier general Frazer received his mortal wound.

The action now became very serious, as the British lines lay exposed to the enemy's sudden attack. In this crisis of danger general Burgoyne appeared cool and intrepid. He directed generals Philips and Reidesel to cover the retreat, while such troops as were most ready were ordered for the defence of the camp. The British troops were hard pressed, but retreated in good order; they were obliged to leave six pieces of cannon behind, all the horses having been killed, and all the artillery men, who had, as usual, behaved with the utmost bravery, being either killed or wounded.

39. John Dyke Acland, major in the 20th Regiment of Foot, commanded the British grenadier battalion in Brugoyne's army.

"Veteran bands
Here made their last campaign."[40]

At the close of evening the troops in action returned with precipitation into camp, pursued and galled. General Burgoyne rode up with evident anxiety to the Quarter Guards,[41] directing Lord Balcarras, the officer commanding, to defend his post to the last extremity. The Americans rushed forward, headed by General Arnold, with an intrepidity which shewed their determined intent to storm the camp. But their General being wounded, they desisted from their object, when dark night appeared, putting her interposing mantle upon bleeding armies.

While the British lines were so boldly attacked, Colonel Breyman, who commanded the Germans was killed, as he bravely defended his post, and the enemy gained an opening on our right and rear. The Germans retreated firing, until they had gained their tents in the rear of the entrenchments; but supposing that the assault was general, gave one discharge, after which some retreated to the British camp, but others surrendered prisoners. Night at length put an end to the engagement.

This day's battle added many brave officers and men to the melancholy list of killed and wounded.[42]

Brigadier general Frazer, on account of his distinguished merit, was greatly lamented by the whole army; Sir James Clarke,[43] general Burgoyne's aid-de-camp, was mortally wounded; majors Ackland and Williams were taken prisoners. The former was wounded. The general himself had some very narrow escapes, a shot passed through his hat and another through his waistcoat. It was with great truth said, that, in the service of this campaign, the British officers bled profusely and most honorably.

40. From Watts, *The celebrated Victory*, 1706.
41. "Quarter guard," a detachment encamped a short distance in front of the main encampment.
42. This was the Battle of Bemis Heights, or the Second Battle of Saratoga.
43. Francis-Carr Clerke, a lieutenant in the 3rd Regiment of Foot Guards, was an aide-de-camp to General Burgoyne.

On the side of the Americans, the loss in killed and wounded was very great, and far exceeded ours.

The enemy now having made a lodgment on the right of the British, their rear of course was exposed.[44] It therefore was evident in such a posture of things, that our position was no longer safe or even tenable, and of consequence orders were given for quitting the ground we occupied, and posting ourselves during the night on the heights. General Burgoyne, by a judicious manœuvre, took a position upon the heights above the general hospital; this was executed in the night with the greatest order, regularity, and silence. By this entire change of front, the American army was under the necessity of forming a new disposition, which rendered a good retreat impracticable.

On the 8th of October, having removed our baggage, and made due preparations, General Burgoyne offered battle, hoping to draw out the Americans on the plain, where veteran and well appointed forces must always prevail over soldiers, such as the Colonial regiments were composed of. Although General Burgoyne invited an engagement, and we expected from the enemy's movements that he would engage, no such favourable opportunity was afforded us. He however, drew up several brigades, and cannonaded us. An howitzer of our's firing short of his lines, the enemy shouted, but another shot, sending a shell in centre of a large column, and doing considerable damage, numbers fled into the woods, and he appeared disposed to attack as it was thought he intended at first.

In the mean time, general Burgoyne discovered that the Americans were marching a strong column forward, in order to turn the British right, which, if effected would have enclosed them on every side; nothing could prevent this but an immediate retreat to Saratoga.

The army began to march to this place at nine o'clock at night; major general Reidesel led the van, and major general Philips brought up the rear. They were under the necessity of leaving the

44. That is, the rear of the British position was susceptible to attack.

sick and wounded behind. Our forces being refreshed and provided with batteaux for the river, began the retreat under the disadvantage of bad weather, and worse roads, until at night we arrived at Saratoga, so fatigued that the soldiers, although wet with the rain, were indisposed to cut wood for fires, and rather desirous to lie down to rest in their drenched cloaths. On the west bank of Hudson's River, near the height of Saratoga, where the British army halted after the retreat, stood general Schuyler's dwelling house, with a range of barracks and store-houses, &c. The evening the army arrived at these buildings, the weather being very wet and cold, the sick and wounded were directed to take possession of these barracks; while the troops took post on the height above it. A little party of us housed in a hen house of General Schuyler, which by some means caught fire, and would have been consumed were it not that some officers who lodged at the General's, perceived the fire, and alarmed us of it. It was with the greatest difficulty that the wounded soldiers were rescued from the flames. The author was in the house when it took fire, and it was with the greatest difficulty that he escaped. Driven from this temporary shelter, the party joined their companions, who were unhoused and exposed to the wet and night air. The bad weather obliged us to abandon our sick and wounded in the hospital tents, but kept back the enemy from galling us in our retreating, as the wetness of the day would stop firing, and confine fighting to the bayonet. This the Colonial army declined, though they were less exhausted than the British.

9TH. This evening the van arrived at the heights of Saratoga, having endured much hardships on the march, from a heavy rain and bad road; here it was discovered that a division of the Americans had already arrived, and were employed in throwing up entrenchments on the heights before the British, on whose approach they retired over the ford, and joined a large body there; who likewise were employed for the same purpose of preventing all retreat.

10TH. The batteaux with what little provisions remained were constantly fired upon, from the opposite side of the river; many of them fell into the hands of the enemy, and several of the men who conducted them, were killed and wounded.

11th. Several men were employed this day in landing the provisions from the boats, and conveying them up to the hill, under a very galling fire from the enemy.

Very great indeed were the distresses which the army had to encounter at this period, yet they were borne with fortitude. The greatest subordination was manifested throughout the British lines. The men were willing and ready to face any danger, when led on by officers whom they loved and respected, and who shared with them in every toil and hardship.

Numerous parties of the militia now joined the Americans and swarmed around the little adverse army like birds of prey. Roaring of cannon and whistling of bullets from their rifle pieces, were heard constantly by day and night.

Here we had three powerful enemies to contend with—Americans—Winter—and Famine.[45] General Gates now manifested his intention of taking advantage from the unfavourable circumstances of our army, by cutting off the means of our procuring provisions, and galling our advanced posts by the American marksmen, who did us great damage. General Burgoyne's dilemma was at this time calamitous, and even desperate. Forsaken by the Indians and Provincial auxiliaries, and reduced in force by continued disasters and losses, to about 3500 effective men, of whom but 2000 were British, he was disabled from retreating, and could entertain not even a forlorn hope of successfully fighting an enemy fourfold in number, and possessing every advantage over him. Yet in this distressing situation British courage suffered no despondency. Some expectation of reinforcements and relief from New York was cherished, and it was generally wished by our troops, that the Americans would make their long menaced attack. In this suspense the army stood the entire day, on the 13th of October, when no prospect of aid arriving,

45. This sentence is from the commonplace book.

or further hopes remaining to withstand the opposing army which almost surrounded us, an account of the provisions was taken, and it was found that we had no subsistence beyond short allowance for three days. On this emergency a council of war was held at which all the Staff and Officers commanding corps assisted, and it was unanimously resolved to treat for a capitulation.

It is a remark which has been frequently made by foreigners of most countries, that there is a feeling, a sensibility observable in the Irish character, which, if not absolutely peculiar to us, forms a most prominent feature in our disposition. The following circumstance, of which many then in the British as well as American armies were witnesses, may not be altogether unappropriate, particularly to the native reader.

During the time of the cessation of arms, while the articles of capitulation were preparing, the soldiers of the two armies often saluted, and discoursed with each other from the opposite banks of the river, (which at Saratoga is about thirty yards wide, and not very deep,) a soldier in the 9th regiment, named Maguire,[46] came down to the bank of the river, with a number of his companions, who engaged in conversation with a party of Americans on the opposite shore. In a short time something was observed very forcibly to strike the mind of Maguire. He suddenly darted like lightning from his companions, and resolutely plunged into the stream. At the very same moment, one of the American soldiers, seized with a similar impulse, resolutely dashed into the water, from the opposite shore. The wondering soldiers on both sides, beheld them eagerly swim towards the middle of the river, where they met; they hung on each others necks and wept; and the loud cries of "my brother! My dear brother!!!" which accompanied the transaction, soon cleared up the mystery, to the astonished spectators. They were both brothers, the first had emigrated from this country, and the other had entered the

46. Patrick McGuire of the 9th Regiment. Muster rolls, 9th Regiment of Foot, WO 12/2653, TNA.

army; one was in the British and the other in the American service, totally ignorant until that hour that they were engaged in hostile combat against each other's life.

CHAPTER SIX

[Imprisoned with the Convention Army]

Captured Troops march to the Vicinity of Boston. Their deplorable Situation. Congress refuses the Embarkation of the British Troops to England. British Troops removed from Prospect-hill to Rutland County. Author made to run the Gauntlet between lines of American Militia near Rutland. Execution of an American Lady and Soldier, together with a British Serjeant and Private, for the Murder of the Lady's Husband.

On the morning of the 17th of October we surrendered, and in the evening crossed the Hudson river from Saratoga on our march to Boston. From the outset of our marching we experienced much hardship, sleeping in barns, and having but bad clothing, and scanty provisions. The way before and about us presented an uncheering appearance, mountainous and barren, with little of pleasing scenery to amuse the traveller. In our progress we crossed the ridge of mountains called *Blue Hills*, which begin in New Hampshire, and extend through a long tract of country in New England. Hadley was the first place we arived at, which had any local attractions to delight the eye. It then consisted of one extensive and spacious street parallel to the river.

From Hadley our rout lay to Prospect-hill, which is about 90 miles distant from it, where we stoped during the winter months, and endured harsh usage in different ways. The people of New England appeared to indulge a deadly hatred against the British prisoners, and rejoiced at any occasion to gratify it. Several of our men were stabbed by the colonial centinels, and one of our officers was shot as he rode in his chaise. We were confined in boarded huts on Winter and Prospect Hills. It is true, the court of Massachusetts passed resolutions for procuring suitable accommodations, but from the general unwillingness of the people to administer the least civility, and from the feebleness of the authority which the American rulers had at that time over the property of their fellow citizens, their situation was rendered truly deplorable.

Such were the disagreeable and distressing circumstances, which on every side increased the miseries of confinement, that, at this time, the most faithful recital must despair of credence. It was not infrequent for thirty, or forty persons, men, women and children, to be indiscriminately crowded together in one small, miserable, open hut. The officers (without any regard to rank), were frequently crowded, six or eight together in one small hut.[1] Our provisions and firewood on short allowance; and a scanty portion of straw their bed, their own blankets their only covering. In the night time, those that could lie down, and the many who sat up from the cold, were obliged frequently to rise and shake from them the snow which the wind drifted in at the openings; or, in case of rain, to endure the "chill peltings of the merciless storm."

While we stopped at Prospect-hill, we often took opportunities to view Bunker's-hill, contiguous to it, on which a desperate action was fought two years before our arrival at the place.

In the Summer of 1778, we were marched by order of Congress from Prospect-hill to Rutland county, which is distant about 50 Miles from Boston.

Seeing that Congress had no intention of allowing the British troops to return to England, according to the articles of convention, and considering myself under no tie of honour, as I gave no parole

1. This sentence is from the commonplace book.

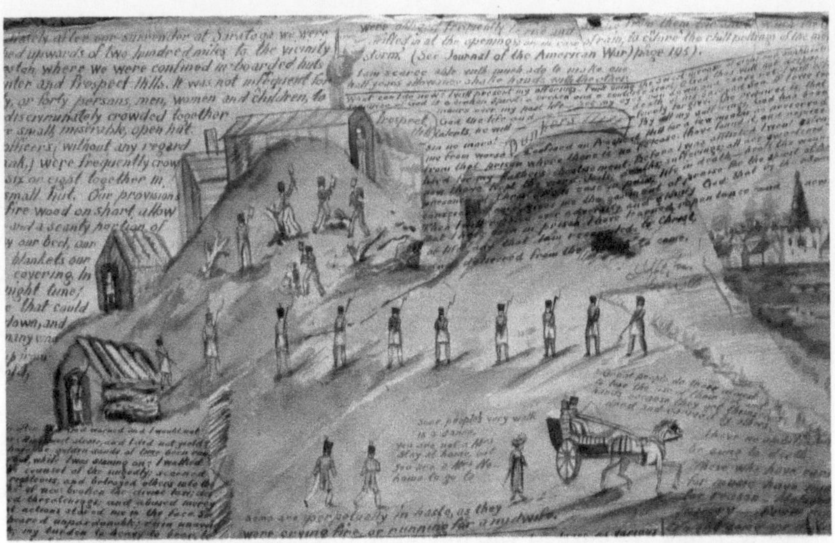

A page from Lamb's commonplace book depicts, in primitive fashion, the crude barracks that housed captured British and German soldiers outside of Boston in the winter of 1777-1778. Prisoners toil to cut firewood while guarded by a line of American soldiers, and townspeople pass by, all clad in the style of the early 1800s. A passage from Lamb's Original and Authentic Journal fills the upper left, while his thoughts on various subjects fill the rest of the space. Methodist Historical Society of Ireland.

(though at that time I was employed as temporary surgeon to the 9th regiment) I resolved to proceed privately to New York. This resolution was confirmed by my meeting at some distance from Prospect-hill, a native of America, for whom I did a kind office, after the battle of Fort-Anne, and from whom I then received an invitation to take refreshment in an adjacent tavern together with a promise of a pasport, which might prevent my being apprehended by the way. Unfortunately there were at that time in the tavern, a few British soldiers who did some damage in the house, and got off without paying for it. The landlord raised the hue and cry against me, although I was in another apartment when the damage was done. He demanded a recompense of 40 dollars to repair his losses, though a small matter, was sufficient to compensate his loss, which consisted but in the breaking of a few drinking glasses.

Having had no part whatever in the affair I naturally refused to comply, and was in consequence taken before a magistrate. However they took the law first into their own hands, as it was agreed that I should run the gauntlet to the magistrate's house, which was about 100 yards from the tavern.[2] Providentially for me the tavern was on a rising ground, and the way I had to run was down a hill which accelerated my motion, so that I received but few blows, although there were a number of persons aiming to strike me as I passed. When I arrived before the magistrate, he in the most unfeeling manner, without hearing my defence, declared if I did not forthwith pay down 40 dollars, he would order me to the prison-ship in Boston, where I should be fed on bread and water. I persisted in declaring I had no part in the outrage, and challenged any person to come forward and prove it against me. My plea was rejected, and to the prison ship I was told I must go, unless I paid the mulct immediately. This I still objected to do. After some consultation among themselves, it was determined that I should run the gauntlet again, which punishment I underwent of course, a number of men taking sticks in their hands, to deal blows at me.

It was an unpleasant atonement on my part for the transgression of others, but I saw I could not avoid it. I was brought to the door and held till my enemies were each man prepared for striking me. The word was given that all was ready, and I was let go from the grasp of the men that held me. I therefore darted along the line with rapidity, and being young and active, I do think, I did not receive in all more than a dozen strokes by reason of their confusion and eagerness to deal blows upon my unprotected head, which by agility and good heels I succeeded in saving. They did not pursue me, and by my rapid marching I was enabled to join my companions. However I felt my body and head sore for many days afterwards.[3]

2. "Gauntlet," a punishment whereby the prisoner ran between two lines of people who were free to strike him.

3. The commonplace book gives the date of this incident as June 24, 1778.

"R. Lamb made to run the gauntlet by the Americans while a prisoner in New England. June 24th 1778." Methodist Historical Society of Ireland.

We arrived in the progress of our march at a township called Rutland. Here we were confined in a sort of penn or fence, which was constructed in the following manner: A great number of trees were ordered to be cut down in the woods, these were sharpened at each end, and drove firmly into the earth very close together, enclosing a space of about two or three acres. American sentinels were planted on the outside of this fence, at convenient distances, in order to prevent our getting out. At one angle, a gate was erected, and on the outside thereof stood the guard house; two sentinels were constantly posted at this gate; and no one could get out unless he had a pass from the officer of the guard; but this was a privilege in which very few were indulged. Boards and nails were given the British in order to make them temporary huts, to secure them from the rain, and the heat of the sun. The provisions were rice and salt pork, delivered with a scanty hand. The officers were allowed to lodge in the farm houses, which lay contiguous to the penn; they were permitted likewise to come in amongst their men for the purpose of roll-call, and other matters of regularity.

During the time of our remaining prisoners at Rutland, a melancholy incident happened, which I consider worthy to be recorded. A serjeant Buchanan received cash from his officer, to provide shoes for the company, but unfortunately squandered it.[4] Apprehensive of punishment, he went away privately, to a place about forty miles from Boston, and worked at his trade to provide as much as he lavished, in order to make good his account. Having saved so much, he was returning to his regiment, and by accident, met with a soldier, who informed him that a serjeant was appointed in his place, it being concluded that he deserted. Being so advised, he resolved to escape to Montreal, (where he left behind him his wife and child) in the hope of obtaining pardon by means of General Sir Guy Carleton, then Governor of Canada. On his route to Canada, he passed though Brookfield, and there, unhappily for the parties, was noticed by a Mrs. Spooner, daughter of General Ruggles,[5] who held a command in the former provincial war. This lady was remarkable for attachment to the Royal cause, although Mr. Spooner was decidedly devoted to the opposite interests. Their difference of thinking produced domestic disagreement, and Mrs. Spooner wickedly meditated the murder of her husband. She actually bribed an American young man to poison him, as he made a journey from home, but fearing that he might escape the ruin so plotted, she disclosed her horrible design to Buchanan, promising him considerable property, and that she herself would accompany him from her abode, on the accomplishment of the murderous conspiracy. Her husband returned safe, and on entering his house discovered Buchanan sitting in the parlour, at which he expressed much displeasure. Although Mrs. Spooner was obliged to send Buchanan to seek another lodging, she secretly communicated with him, and although Buchanan

4. Serjeant James Buchanan of the 9th Regiment, born in Glasgow in 1742, left his family in Canada when he went on Burgoyne's expedition. Navas, *Murdered By His Wife*, 111.
5. Timothy Ruggles, a Massachusetts loyalist who followed the British army when they left Boston. His daughter Bathsheba married Joshua Spooner.

afterward alledged, that he shrank from perpetrating the murder, he actually consented in the terrible plot, for the purpose of obtaining a share of the property which he expected would be the reward of its execution. At this unhappy juncture of inhuman contrivance, a soldier named Brooks (whom the Author mentioned to have jumped over board, on the voyage to America, through fear of being punished for stealing an article of wearing apparel) happened to travel through the town, and from his daring character, was taken by Buchanan into a partnership of the intended dreadful transaction. Mr. Spooner, having gone some distance from home in the day, it was determined to dispatch him on his return at night. Brooks was selected as the executioner, who waited in a convenient corner near the door, and actually fractured the skull of the ill-fated gentleman, with a log of wood, as he made his entrance. The party then plundered the house of cash, and Buchanan, Brooks and the American, departed to divide and spend their booty in safety. The body however was discovered thrown down in a deep draw-well, and Mrs. Spooner, on examination, confessed the abominable deed which originated in her own wickedness. The party who fled were followed, secured, and, together with Mrs. Spooner, soon after brought to trial, and deservedly sentenced to suffer death.[6] Buchanan was deeply impressed with the justice of the capital atonement they were doomed to make, and by his means chiefly, his guilty partners became truly penitent. Buchanan addressed letters to his officers, full of religious contrition, and the Author of this Memoir by desire of his officers visited them, and was present at the hour of their being executed. The awfulness of it was great indeed, and the truly contrite feelings of the culprits were calculated to turn vicious spectators to virtuous and pious ways. Mrs. Spooner, however, indulged hopes to the last of escaping condign punishment, pleaded pregnancy as an argument for being respited, and

6. The full story of this murder and the trial is in Navas, *Murdered By His Wife.*

seemed impenitent a good deal. One thing respecting Brooks, was somewhat astonishing. Before the perpetration of the horrid plot for which he suffered, he was notoriously prophane, and almost illiterate. But during his confinement, and the interval of the preparation for death allowed after trial, he attended so much to a devout perusal of the Holy Scriptures, that he could read the Sacred Volume with facility, explain it to his unhappy companions in an edifying manner, and even select the chapters most appropriate to their sad condition. The time of execution appeared marked with horror suited to the awful scene. The malefactors had to pass two miles to the gallows, and, although the former part of the day was serene and fine, of a sudden, as they approached the place, the sky was covered with clouds, and a storm of thunder followed with copious rain, attached additional terrors to their ignominious catastrophe.

CHAPTER SEVEN

[First Escape to New York]

The Author makes his escape into New York. His Narrative.

THE CAPTURED TROOPS IN New England were ordered to march to the east parts of Virginia. This was universally considered by the privates as a very great hardship, and by the officers as a shameful violation of the articles of capitulation.

When I saw that the American rulers had no intention of allowing the British troops to return to England, I determined on attempting my escape into New York. The idea immediately suggested itself to me, that it would be much more agreeable, and indeed less dangerous, to have companions in my flight; I therefore resolved to induce as many of my comrades as I could to join me. I soon made myself acquainted with the route which it was necessary that we should take; I found that we were to cross the North River,[1] only sixty or seventy miles above New York. This then appeared to me the most favorable point from which to attempt our escape. Unfortunately, however, for my scheme, our officers (fearful of their regiments being, at their return to Europe, reduced to mere skeletons) had previously issued orders, that if any soldier should absent himself from his regiment only for one day or night, he should be

1. The Hudson River.

returned as a deserter; and if brought back to his regiment by any of the inhabitants or American soldiers, he should be tried by a court martial, and punished accordingly. I was fully aware, that the intention of this order was to keep the men together, and likewise to deter them from remaining in the country, it being the constant practice of the Americans to induce the captive soldiers to become settlers. These orders prevented many from attempting their escape. But for them, numbers like myself, and the companions of my journey, would have made good their escape into New York.

While the Americans protected to the uttermost those deserters, who left the British army to settle among them, they who were caught by them in the attempt to join the King's forces at New York, had every thing to fear; nor was the least their being brought back to their respective regiments under the odium of desertion.

I weighed in my mind all the consequences that would most probably result, should I be taken by the natives; and the more I thought of the attempt, the more I began to feel a degree of enthusiasm, to which I was before a stranger. I looked forward, not without hope, to the prospects before me, and I began already to indulge the exultation of effecting my escape. Indeed I had wrought myself up to such a pitch of firmness, that I am persuaded, the most agonizing cruelties which the Americans could have inflicted on my body, would have been unable to have effected any alteration in my resolution.

I communicated my scheme to two of my comrades, over whom I had most influence, and persuaded them to join me in the attempt; one of these soldiers understanding the French and German languages, was a powerful assistant in effecting our escape, as our guards were chiefly composed of German troops.[2] By his conversing with these men, we obtained permission to go to a house in order to buy some necessaries which we wanted. When we got to the

2. "German troops," men from German states who had settled in the colonies and were serving in the Continental Army.

house, we took care not to return to the line of centries again; but moved further from the guards, by degrees; until we entirely lost sight of them. We then began to fear, lest the next inhabitants we met, might pick us up and bring us back. We therefore thought it best to conceal ourselves. Just at this critical moment, we perceived a small hut on the verge of a wood. On our entering it, we found a poor woman with two children. We entreated her to hide us for a few hours, as we were apprehensive that the American soldiers would soon miss us, follow, and make search for us. As the chief inducement to obtain her assistance, we immediately shewed her some silver money, which we promised to give her, if she assisted us in making our escape. To this she readily consented, and as a pledge of sincerity left her little child with us. She gave us some provisions, locked us all up in a small apartment, and went out in order to gain information. There was a characteristic shrewdness about this woman which highly fitted her for our purpose. She very acutely observed, before she went, that this would be the best method, for if our pursuers should come to the house, and observe it fastened up, they would not, she believed, break it open, unless they had some previous information of our being concealed there; and as nobody had observed our coming into the hut, she hoped there would be no danger.

In this place we remained until dark, under the unpleasant apprehension of being seized every moment by our pursuers, as we were in the very midst of them; however, fortunately for us, not one of them either knocked at the door or demanded entrance.

The woman returned in the evening. "You see," said she, "that I have been faithful to you. Your comrades have all crossed the North River, with most of their guards, and there are very few of the Americans at this side of the river." It may be naturally supposed that we all felt ourselves much indebted to her for her faithfulness; and, as far as was in our power, we rewarded her. We then informed her, that we intended to make our escape into New York. She observed, that that would be a very hard task to accomplish, as there were several American encampments in the Highlands, which lay between us and that city. However she gave us a recommendation to a man living a few miles off, who, she observed, would assist us in getting forward. Taking an affectionate leave of our faithful hostess, we directed our course to the house of her friend; but before we had proceeded three miles, we were stopped by a deep and rapid stream. My comrades not knowing how to swim I proposed to swim across, taking one of them at a time with me, if they would faithfully and courageously follow my advice, which was to lay their hands gently on my loins while in the water, striking out with their feet at the same time. This method would have soon carried us all across, as the river was not very broad; however they both declined it, as too hazardous an attempt, and proposed to trace the river upwards, in order to discover a fording place. We had not proceeded up the river two hundred yards, when we perceived a tree lying across the stream; this served the inhabitants for a bridge. Such conveniences for passing rivers are very common in America. We crossed the river in safety, and pursuing our journey, arrived at the house to which we had been directed by our late kind hostess. It stood alone at the edge of a wood, and being unconnected with any other human dwelling, seemed admirably adapted to our purpose. The family were much alarmed when we rapped them up.[3] We, however, soon made the owner acquainted with our intentions, and informed him, that if he would conduct us to New York, we would give him twenty dollars, exclusive of the reward he would receive from the commander in chief. He listened with attention, and seemed willing to comply; but his wife, overhearing our discourse, opposed it immediately, and declared, with tears in her eyes, that he should not go. The rude reasonings of this woman appeared so powerful an instance of conjugal feeling, that they made a strong impression on my mind at the time. To the married reader little apology is due for their introduction. "What!" said she, "do you mean to break my

3. "Rapped them up," woke them by knocking on the door.

heart, by foolishly running into the jaws of death, depriving me of a husband, and my children of a father? You know that there are several camps and garrisons between this and New York, that you would not be able to go ten miles before you would be taken up, and then you would be hung up like a dog." This discourse operated with all the power of simple nature, when the whole force of the passions is brought to bear on any given point. The man changed his mind in a moment. "Gentlemen," said he, "this is a very dangerous piece of work; I know that all my wife has said is true; I know that the Americans have very strong out-posts all along the North River, as far as King's Bridge, and if I were taken in the act of bringing you into the British lines, I could expect no mercy." All our arguments after this, could not prevail with him, though we promised to give him twelve dollars in advance, and two new English blankets; however he at last, for a small present, conducted us to another friend, who lived two miles further on our journey; this person, he observed, might probably go with us.

We set off between one and two o'clock in the morning and arrived at the poor man's hut, which was situated on the top of a high mountain. When we entered the hut, we found his wife ill of a fever, and the husband, with a woman, attending bed. After much persuasion, and a small present, we prevailed with this man to bring us to another friend that lived six miles onwards, and whom there was every probability we might obtain for a guide. We set off immediately, and after making our way for six hours, through a trackless desert, full of swamps, we found ourselves at day-break very near the out-posts of an American encampment. Here our guide, on finding where we were, being much terrified, fled from it with the greatest precipitation. As his last act of attention, he pointed out a path-way which led into the woods, and told us to pursue that track, and it would bring us to a friend. We took his advice, and continued on that track for five or six miles, when we came to a small hut. The inhabitants were astonished at our appearance, but evidently pleased at our company. We informed the woman that we were very hungry.

She immediately prepared a repast for us, which I need not add, was at that time highly acceptable, as we had not eaten any thing for the space of forty-eight hours.

The fatigue we had underdone during our march, from the extent of country which we had traversed, rendered sleep highly necessary, and we prepared to lie down. This measure the woman warmly opposed. She said, "the American soldiers often straggled from their camp to her hut, and some of them might probably come upon it while we slept." Her husband now came in, and seemed glad to see us. We made him acquainted with our intention of escaping into New York. He repeated the observations of our other directors, relative to the number of the American posts, particularly on the North River; and added, "that it would be an hundred chances to one, if we were not taken." We told him that we would reward him liberally, if he would conduct us. He answered, "There is a young man who lives several miles off, who will, I believe, undertake it: if he should, I have no objection to go; but I will not go by myself, as I well know the dangers which we shall be exposed to without a second guide."

We remained at this place two days, encouraging them by every argument which we could suggest to make the attempt. At last we prevailed, by giving them ten dollars and the two new English blankets, which we had with us. We set off with our two guides about six o'clock in the evening, and after travelling through deep swamps, thick woods, and over difficult mountains for ten hours, our young guide stopped, and declared that he would not proceed any further with us, unless we gave him forty dollars in hand. He said, "This is a dangerous, troublesome piece of work. Here," continued he, "is an American encampment within a mile of us; I have been there a few days ago, and I know where all the centries are posted; if I should be taken, I shall lose my life." As he uttered this, he seemed to be under great terror and fear, which increased when we said, "We are not afraid of one or two American centinels, only conduct us the best way you can; and if we unavoidably fall in with any of them, you may leave the matter to us and fly for your life." All we could say had no effect on him, and although we offered him on the spot twelve dollars, he would not advance one step further. We then encouraged our other guide to proceed with us, to which, after much entreaty and promises of reward, he consented.

We expected every moment, as we advanced, to fall in with the line of centries belonging to the Americans; but, happily for us, as it rained very hard during the whole night, and was very dark, we did not encounter one of them, though we passed very near to a log house, which was full of troops. Taking, however, every possible precaution, we immediately struck off into the woods, and after climbing up precipices, and wading through swamps, about five o'clock in the morning, we arrived at the wished for house. This was situated only two miles from another encampment. Our guide being well acquainted with this family, told them who we were, and also our intention. They received us very kindly, and gave us refreshment, informing us, at the same time, that it would be highly dangerous for us to remain in the house, as the American soldiery were scattered over almost the whole face of the country. We held a consultation what was to be done under the then existing circumstances; and it was unanimously agreed, that we should hide ourselves in a hay-stack, which was near the house, until our guide could explore the country, and find out the safest way for our escape. We were conducted to the spot on which it stood, when each of us buried himself up to the chin in the hay, and waited the event. Our conductor was vigilant in procuring all the intelligence he could with regard to the station of the American army. This delayed him much longer than we at first imagined. Our not hearing aught from him during the space of thirty hours, made us very uneasy; we were fearful lest he also had forsaken us, and left us to shift for ourselves. At last he came, and had us prepare to follow him. We were at that time about forty miles from King's Bridge, the out post of the British army. Thus circumstanced, we determined to accomplish the march, if possible, that night; we therefore set off in high spirits, about six o'clock in the evening.

Previous to the commencement of our journey, we were informed by our guide of our perilous situation, while we remained concealed in the hay-stack. The Americans had determined to remove it to the camp for forage, which probably would have been done the day before, only that it rained remarkably hard during the whole of it. Fortunately for us, the storm continued, with unabated violence, all night; and the darkness was such, that we were completely shrouded from all observation. These circumstances tended very much to favor our escape.

After as hard a march as any poor fellows ever experienced for the time, over swamps, rivers, and mountains, we arrived a little before day-light at a small house about one mile from the British outposts at King's Bridge, fifteen miles from New York. We boldly rapped at the door, and demanded entrance. The inhabitants were much terrified, on our approach, and their fears began sensibly to increase, when we ordered them to light a candle. They assured us, that if a light were seen in their house, at that hour, the habitation would be soon tumbled about their ears, for the British fort would immediately fire into it; we were, therefore, constrained to remain in that situation until day-light had commenced, as it would have been highly dangerous to have proceeded to the fort in the dark. Soon as morning dawned we left the house, and with joyful hearts proceeded to the fort. The out-centry challenged us; we answered, "We are British soldiers, who have made good our escape." We were conducted with joy and wonder to the fort, and received with great kindness by the officers and men. I believe we were the first party belonging to general Burgoyne's army, that effected an escape.[4] It would not be very easy to give the reader an adequate idea, either of my own feelings, or those of my associates on this occasion. The toil and hardships we had sustained, the dangers which we had sur-

4. Other soldiers of Burgoyne's army had made their escape sooner, but Lamb was among the first to get to New York by way of the Hudson River. See Richard Sampson, *Escape in America: the British Convention Prisoners, 1777-1783* (Chippenham, UK: Picton Publishing, 1995).

mounted; captivity, or death, in its most frightful shapes, every moment presenting horrid images to our minds; in avoiding destruction or recapture from the Americans, encountering the hazard of still greater calamities; sinking into the morass or quagmire; drowning in the rapid torrent; tumbling headlong from the dreadful precipice; not to mention the terrors of the woods, among which, the least was the encountering the venomous bite of the American serpents: when delivered from all these, we joined our countrymen and fellow soldiers in arms. Such a moment must be imagined; it cannot be described.

We were, of course, immediately conducted forward to New York. We arrived at New York 25th Nov. 1778, when major Andre,[5] the adjutant general, received us with great affability and kindness, at the head quarters. As I was the person who first planned the means of escape, and conducted the whole plan, under the guides, I was the object to which every inquiry was directed. Sir Henry Clinton the commander in chief, was an experienced officer, and a sensible man. He, doubtless, gave private orders, relative to my examination, willing to gain information of every circumstance, however minute, that might (by communicating intelligence of the state of the country,) add to the security of the British army. I am also inclined to think, that much of the bounty that I and my comrades received, was the result of Sir Henry's secret benevolence. Major Andre immediately brought me into the parlour, inquired very minutely into every circumstance of the route I had taken with my party, and the dangers I was exposed to: the number of the enemy, the usage which the British soldiers received when prisoners, &c. &c. &c. When I had given him all the information which I could, he expressed much satisfaction, and told me, that if I chose, I might take my passage to England in the next packet, that sailed {as I was at that time a non-commissioned officer, I had the privilege of being sent home}; but, at the same time, he intimated a wish that I would

5. John André, adjutant general to the British army in New York, later executed as a spy.

continue to serve in America. I answered, "That I would rather remain, and serve his majesty in America, than go home to England."

The major then, with much feeling and politeness, informed me, that he was authorized by Sir Henry Clinton, to offer me my choice of entering in any regiment, then serving in America. I came to the resolution of serving in the 23d, or Royal Welch Fuzileers, then quartered in New York. I was soon after appointed serjeant by colonel, now general Balfour, to whose kind attention I must ever feel myself much indebted.[6] I was immediately sent to an officer*, who was appointed to pay the men who made their escape from confinement, the usual bounty. The distinction made in cases like mine, by general Burgoyne himself, was highly flattering to the military feelings of the soldier. The general used to term them, "honorable desertions." This distinction he made, even in the house of commons, between these soldiers, who, through every difficulty, made their way to, and joined his majesty's forces, and those who left their regiments, for the purpose of settling among the Americans.

It was, no doubt, truly pleasing to regain my liberty, and join my friends and fellow-soldiers in New York, after the hardships and sufferings we endured since our becoming prisoners at Saratoga. It was about this period of the war that Harry Calvert, Esq.[7] now Lieutenant General and Adjutant General of the British forces, joined our Regiment. I remember that I was the serjeant appointed

*Colonel Handfield, the present commissary general of Ireland. [Editor: Charles Handfield had held a number of staff positions during the war in America including "Paymaster of the Absent Corps", and was responsible for settling the accounts of escaped prisoners who came into New York. He was Commissary General in Ireland until 1822.]

---

6. Three men from the 9th Regiment were added to the rolls of the 23rd on December 1, 1778: Roger Lamb, Abraham Gartside and William Gunn. Presumably the latter two were Lamb's companions on his escape; later evidence recorded by Lamb indicates that Gunn was the man who spoke French and German. Lamb was appointed corporal in the 23rd on October 25, 1779, and sergeant on April 29, 1780. Muster rolls, 23rd Regiment of Foot, WO 12/3960, TNA.

7. Harry Calvert obtained a commission in the 23rd Regiment of Foot on April 24, 1778.

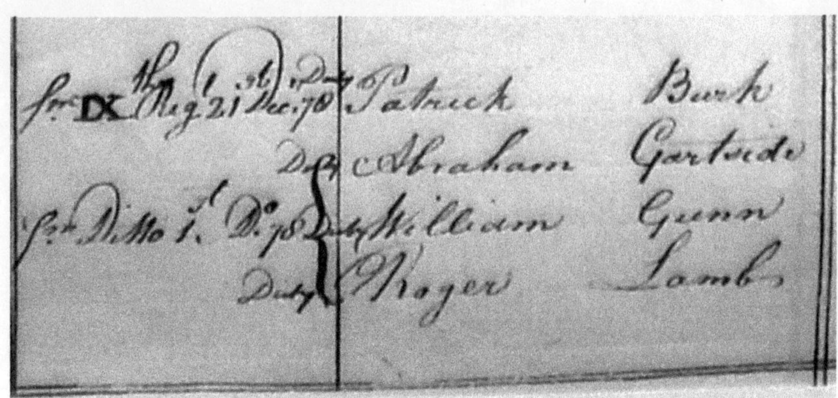

Detail of the muster roll showing Lamb's enlistment into the 23rd Regiment of Foot. WO 12/3960, The National Archives.

to the first guard which he mounted after joining us. At that early age he exhibited specimens of the ability and professional knowledge which raised him to the high rank he holds in the service. The Author has derived peculiar advantage from his kind condescension, in recognising him after a lapse of years since he fought by his side, and had the gratification of being particularly noticed by him for soldierly conduct in action. General Calvert was from the outset of his military life, endeared to the men under his command, and it ought to be mentioned to his honour that he always appeared pleased on any occasion of benefiting an old soldier for his past services.

CHAPTER EIGHT

[Southern Campaign, 1780]

Connecticut Expedition. Sir Henry Clinton, with a large Body of Troops sails from New York, and arrives, after much Difficulty, in South Carolina. Charlestown Capitulates to the British Forces. Sir Henry Clinton returns to New York. Lord Cornwallis takes the Command of the Royal Forces in the Southern Provinces. Battle near Camden.

THE PROVINCE OF CONNECTICUT was the great source from whence the Americans recruited their armies and supplied them with provisions. It had, from its situation, hitherto sustained little of that rage of war, which most of the other provinces had endured. The British commander, to convince the inhabitants that their province was not inaccessible, and that it was to our lenity, and forbearance they were indebted, planned an expedition against it. It formed also part of the general's plan, to compel Washington to quit his strong situation on the North River, and descend into the country, for the defence of the sea coast.

As this expedition has been greatly misrepresented, both by Ramsay and Belsham, the Author takes the liberty to transcribe from his Journal the following account of this affair, as he was himself personally employed on the service.[1] He is happy to state, that

1. David Ramsay, *History of the American Revolution* (Philadelphia: R. Aitken & Son, 1789),

many respectable British officers are still living, (particularly general Garth, second in command on the expedition,)[2] who can bear full accord to the truth of the following account. Indeed such refutation becomes the more necessary, as the British army still lies under the odium thrown on it by those virulent party writers, which has never yet, to the Author's knowledge, been answered by any one.

The transports, on board which were troops amounting to two thousand six hundred men, weighed anchor at the entrance into the sound, and sailed towards New Haven, the capital of Connecticut, the 4th of July. Major general Tryon commanded the land forces.[3] Commodore Sir George Collier, in the Camille frigate, with the Scorpion sloop, Halifax brig, and Hussar galley, was appointed to the naval command, and escorted the transports. The first division of the troops, under brigadier general Garth, of the guards, disembarked at some distance below the town of New Haven. He had to pass the head of a creek, and was in consequence compelled to take a march of seven miles, amidst the. continued opposition of the inhabitants; he, nevertheless, forced his way, and succeeded in gaining possession of the town. Meanwhile major general Tryon, with the 2d division, landed on the opposite side of the harbour, and took a fort on the heights, the artillery of which commanded it; direct communication was thus established between the two divisions of the army, one of which was in possession of the town. The vessels in the harbour, artillery, ammunition, public stores, &c. were taken or destroyed; but, notwithstanding the opposition of the inhabitants, and their even firing from the windows, after the troops were in possession of the town, such was the British humanity, that, instead of indiscriminate death, which by the laws of war they were liable to, the town was saved from damage, and private houses, as much as possible, exempted from plunder, by placing sentinels before

and William Belsham, *Memoirs of the Reign of George III to the Session of Parliament 1793* (G.G. and James Robinson, 1795).

2. Brigadier General George Garth of the Brigade of Guards.

3. William Tryon, the royal governor of New York, also held a commission as a major general.

them, many of whom, (such was the American gratitude,) were actually wounded on their posts! The next day a proclamation was issued, promising protection and pardon to all who should return to their allegiance, and threatening to punish as traitors those who did not. The fort was then dismantled; the troops were re-embarked, and New Haven was left in a far better situation than many less offending places have experienced in all countries during war.

The expedition next proceeded to Fairfield. After the landing of the troops, the opposition from the inhabitants was far more desperate than at New Haven. The lenity already shewn to the offenders, serving only to make them more outrageous, an example of severity became indispensible. All the public stores, and the vessels in the harbour, were therefore either taken or destroyed, and the town itself was laid in ashes. This example had not its desired effect. As the troops proceeded, the opposition became more determined, and of a nature which no regular army could patiently endure: no established system of warfare pardon. Norwark and Greenfield,[4] places taken immediately afterward, therefore underwent a similar fate.

New London, the rendezvous for the American privateers, was the last place, the reduction of which general Tryon had in view; but as still more obstinate resistance was apprehended there, it was judged that a supply of ammunition, and an augmentation of troops should be obtained before it was attacked, though the loss of the British in the expedition amounted only to twenty killed, ninety-six wounded, and thirty-two missing. The fleet, therefore, returned to Huntington Bay, in Long Island.

Such is the simple, impartial, and unbiassed narrative of an expedition, which Ramsay, and after him Belsham, have endeavoured, with all the artifice of wilful misrepresentation, so to colour as to render the British name odious to humanity. No doubt, in such excursions many scenes occur, at which the feeling heart must revolt;

4. Norwalk and Ridgefield, Connecticut.

but in war, all that the brave and the humane can do, is to soften and alleviate its horrors; to prevent them entirely, is altogether beyond the power of man. And that this was done almost in every point, by the commanding officers, the Author can aver from his own personal knowledge. But if persons, whose residence unfortunately becomes the seat of war, will not govern themselves prudently, whom have they to blame, except themselves, for all the disastrous consequences that may ensue?

Mr. Ramsay makes the strange assertion, that at New Haven "the inhabitants were stripped of their houshold furniture and other moveable property; and the harbour and water-side were covered with feathers, which were discharged from opened beds!" Strange, indeed, that soldiers weighed down with arms, ammunition, and provisions, should carry feather beds so far to destroy them! and as for the houshould furniture what were they to do with it? Such slanderous improbabilities refute themselves: I never saw any thing of the kind. But further, he has the hardihood to assert, that "an aged citizen, who laboured under a natural inability of speech, had his tongue cut out by one of the royal army;" and that "a sucking infant was plundered of part of its clothing, while a bayonet was presented to the breast of its mother." It is literally impossible for one who has been in America during great part of the war, and who has actually fought in several of the engagements, to read such gross falsehoods without feeling more indignation than he can readily express, and heaving a sigh for the depravity of human nature. I am certain, that either of these actions, proved on a British soldier, would have been punished by his officers with the greatest severity.

Mr. Belsham, although somewhat more cautious and guarded in his assertions than Ramsay, is equally rancorous; and from the art with which he fabricates his deceptions, is a far more dangerous writer. His allusion to the words of the proclamation, that "the existence of a single house on the coast, was a striking monument of British mercy," is highly uncandid. This was an act of mercy after their cruel behaviour to the troops. And the assertion that "all the buildings and farm houses for two miles in extent round the town, were laid in ashes," I can take upon me to contradict as a gross and malignant falshood. And yet these are the men who assume the pompous name of historians, and who transmit the most wanton misrepresentations of public events, together with the most wicked slander of illustrious individuals, to generations yet unborn!

Towards the latter end of the year 1779, Sir Henry Clinton entrusted the command of the royal army in New York, to lieutenant general Knyphausen,[5] and embarked for the southward, with a formidable force, provisions, ammunition, &c. The whole sailed from Sandy Hook on the 26th of December, under convoy of admiral Arbuthnot.[6] The passage proved both tedious and dangerous. Part of the ordnance, some of the artillery, and most of the cavalry horses were lost; nor did the fleet arrive at Tybu,[7] in Georgia, until the 31st of January, 1780.

In a few days the transports sailed with the army for North Edisto. They landed about thirty miles from Charlestown (after a short passage) and took possession of John's Island, Stono ferry, James's Island, and Wappo-cut. A bridge being thrown over the canal, part of the force took post on the banks on Ashley river, opposite Charlestown.

The tedious passage from New York, afforded opportunity to the Americans to fortify Charlestown; and from the losses which the expedition had sustained, Sir Henry Clinton deemed it prudent to send orders to New York for a reinforcement of men and stores. He also drew twelve hundred men from the garrison at Savannah. Brigadier general Patterson[8] who commanded this detachment, crossed the river Savannah, and traversing the country, arrived on

5. Wilhelm von Knyphausen lieutenant general of the German forces serving with the British army in America.

6. Mariot Arbuthnot, vice admiral commanding the British naval forces in America.

7. Tybee, Georgia.

8. James Paterson, lieutenant colonel of the 63rd Regiment of Foot and brigadier general in America.

A sergeant in the 23rd Regiment of Foot, Royal Welch Fusiliers, as he may have looked in New York City in 1779. The black bearskin cap was characteristic of fusilier regiments, but may not have been in use at this time. His clothing is of finer material than the private soldiers', and his rank is indicated by a red sash with a dark blue stripe matching the lapel color. The coat buttons may have been of a different style, plated with silver, and the buttonholes are trimmed with white braid. He wears gloves, and over his shoes are short black canvas spatterdashes. The ornate sword is based on a surviving example, and hangs from a waistbelt worn over the shoulder that also supports a bayonet scabbard hidden from view. Illustration by Eric Schnitzer.

the banks of Ashley river. The siege was immediately commenced. A depot was formed at Wappo, on James's Island; fortifications were erected there, and on the main land, opposite the southern and western ends of Charlestown. An advanced party crossed the river, and broke ground at eight hundred yards from the American works; and batteries were erected on Charlestown neck. Nor were the Americans idle during this period: they put the town into every possible state of defence.

On the day of our arrival at John's Island, near Charlestown, I was sent on a command with the chief Engineer to explore whether or not the river was navigable for provision-boats. We proceeded in the interior to a plantation, on which I addressed a working-slave, who actually appeared so rude and debared from civilizing intercourse, that the unfortunate human creature could not make himself intelligible to us in English. He seemed to converse with his fellow negroes in a barbarous giberish which evidently was never improved by learned men, to entitle it to the distinction of what ought to be called a language. The condition of this inhumanly oppressed race of men was then in several, and still continues in some of the Southern States of North America distressful in the extreme. It is honourable to the British empire to have abolished this disgraceful tyranny in her own territorial dependencies, and to discourage it by all means among the nations with who she cultivates the relations of amity and peace.

The British troops carried on their parallel[9] from the 3d to the 10th of April. Immediately on the completion of the first parallel, the town was summoned to surrender; the batteries were opened;[10] and from that time, a constant fire commenced. On the Wando River, at Simpson's Port, and Santie Ferry, posts were established, and works thrown up by the Americans, to guard their reinforcements and secure their retreat.

9. "Parallels," fortified trenches built to face an enemy fortification.

10. "Opened," commenced firing.

Meanwhile, admiral Arbuthnot passed Fort Moultrie, on Sullivan's Island, though strongly opposed from the American batteries, and anchored under James's Island, with the loss of twenty-seven seamen killed and wounded, some damage to the shipping, and the burning of the Acteus transport, which grounded within gun shot of the island. The American commander, with his fleet, fell back to Charlestown.

The Americans, to keep up the communication with the country, formed a camp at Monk's Corner, which was the rendezvous of their militia. This post was surprized by lieutenant colonel Tarleton,[11] which gave the British the command of the country, and enable them to intercept the supplies of provisions.

Our batteries soon obtained a superiority over those of the enemy, a council of war was held by the Americans, in consequence of which, the town offered to surrender, on condition of "security to the persons and property of the inhabitants, and leave being given for the Americans to withdraw."

These terms were instantly rejected by general Clinton, as soon as they were offered; but the garrison would not alter their conditions, under the hope that succours would soon arrive from the neighbouring states, in consequence of which, the town was closely invested, both by land and water, Fort Moultrie surrendered, and the American cavalry, which had escaped from Monk's Corner were all either killed, captured, or dispersed.

On the 9th of May, the town was again summoned, and Lincoln[12] was inclined to surrender his army prisoners of war; but the inhabitants thought to obtain better terms, and the siege recommenced. The third parallel was opened, shells and carcasses[13] thrown into the town, and the cannon and mortars played on the garrison at less than one hundred yards distance; the pickets, crossed the

11. Banastre Tarleton, commander of the British Legion, a loyalist regiment.
12. Benjamin Lincoln, commander of the American garrison in Charleston.
13. "Carcass," an incendiary projectile fired from a mortar.

ditch by sap,[14] and advanced within twenty-five yards of the American works.

Matters continued in this state till the 11th, when the inhabitants addressed general Lincoln to capitulate, which was accordingly done, and major general Leslie[15] took possession of the town on the 12th. There were in it upwards of four hundred pieces of artillery. The garrison, as prisoners of war, marched out of the town; their drums were not allowed to beat a British march, nor their colours to be uncased.[16] They laid down their arms in front of the works; the militia returned home, on parole; the inhabitants were considered as prisoners on parole, and like the militia, held their property accordingly; a vessel was allowed to proceed to Philadelphia, with general Lincoln's dispatches, unopened; upwards of five thousand troops, and near one thousand sailors surrendered; all the ships of war, and other vessels were taken.

Sir Henry Clinton (leaving between three and four thousand men for the southern service) embarked early in June for New York. On his departure the command devolved on earl Cornwallis.

In the mean time the Americans marched an army through Jersey and Pennsylvania, and thence proceeded toward South Carolina. As the American army approached to South Carolina, our army, which then consisted of seventeen hundred infantry, and two hundred cavalry was concentrated at Camden. The army with which General Gates advanced, was by the arrival of the militia, increased nearly to six thousand men. On the night of the 15th [of August] we marched from Camden, intending to attack the Americans in their camp at Rugeley's Mills. In the same night Gates put his army in motion, with an intention of surprising our camp, or posting himself on an eligible position near Camden. Our army was ordered to

14. "Saps," trenches which ran forwards towards an enemy fortification.
15. Alexander Leslie, lieutenant colonel of the 64th Regiment of Foot and major general in America.
16. "Colours to be uncased," flags of the surrendered American regiments were on their poles but wrapped in protective cases instead of being unfurled.

march at ten o'clock P. M. The American army was ordered to march at the same hour. The advance guard of both armies met about two o'clock in the morning. Some of the American cavalry, being wounded in the first fire fell back on others, who recoiled so suddenly, that the first Maryland regiment was broken, and the whole line of their army was thrown into confusion. The enemy soon rallied and both they and we kept our ground, and a few shots only from the advanced centries of each army were fired during the night. A colonel Patterfield,[17] on whose abilities general Gates particularly depended, was wounded in the early part of this skirmish. As soon as day light appeared, we saw at a few yards distance our enemy drawn up in very good order in three lines. Our little army was formed in the following plan:

Four companies of light infantry, Royal Welch Fusileers, or 23d regiment, on the right wing, led on by lieutenant colonel Webster.

Volunteers of Ireland, Legion Infantry, two American loyal corps, on the left wing, led on by lord Rawdon.

Two six and two three pounders were placed in the centre, between the two wings.

71st, the Legion cavalry regiment, with two six pounders, formed the reserve.

It happened that the ground on which both armies stood, was narrowed by swamps on the right and left, so that the Americans could not avail themselves of their superior numbers in out flanking us. We immediately began the attack with great vigor, and in a few minutes the action became general along the whole line; there was a dead calm with a little haziness in the air, which prevented the smoke from rising; this occasioned such thick darkness, that it was difficult to see the effect of the fire on either sides. Our army either kept up a constant fire, or made use of their bayonets as opportunity offered. After an obstinate resistance for some time the Americans were thrown into total confusion, and were forced to give way in all

17. Charles Porterfield, lieutenant colonel of a Virginia regiment.

quarters. The continental troops behaved well, but some of the militia were soon broken. In justice to the North Carolina militia, it should be remarked, that part of the brigade commanded by general Gregory[18] acquitted themselves well; they were formed immediately on the left of the continentals, and kept the field while they had a cartridge to fire. Gregory himself was twice wounded by a bayonet in bringing off his men: several of his regiment, and many of his brigade who were made prisoners had no wound except from bayonets. About one thousand prisoners were taken, two hundred and ninety of which being wounded were carried into Camden, and more than twice that number killed. The Americans lost the whole of their artillery, eight brass field pieces, upward of two hundred waggons, and the greatest part of their baggage, tents, &c. with a number of colors. Almost all their officers were separated from their respective commands. The fugitives who fled on the common road, were pursued above twenty miles by colonel Tarleton's cavalry, and the way was covered with arms, baggage, and waggons. Baron de Kalb, the second in command, a brave and experienced officer in the American service, was mortally wounded, having exhibited great gallantry in the course of the action, and received eleven wounds; he was taken prisoner, and died on the next day of his wounds; we buried him in Camden with all the honors of war.

As in this engagement, I had the honor of carrying one standard of colours belonging to the 23d regiment,[19] I was of course, near the centre of the right wing. I had an opportunity of beholding the behaviour of both the officers and privates; it was worthy the character of the British troops. The recollection still dwells deeply in my memory. Lord Cornwallis's judgment in planning, his promptitude in executing, and his fortitude and coolness during the time of action, justly attracted universal applause and admiration. The earl of

18. Isaac Gregory, brigadier general of the North Carolina militia.
19. Each British regiment had two colors, or flags, normally carried by ensigns; apparently a shortage of officers prompted them to be carried by a serjeant on this occasion.

Moira, (then lord Rawdon, who was only twenty-five years of age)[20] bore a very conspicuous part in the contest. Colonel Webster also ought to be particularly mentioned. His conduct was completely consistent with his general character in the army. Cool, determined, vigilant, and active; he added to a reputation established by long service the universal esteem and respect of the whole army, as an officer, whose experience and observation were equal to his personal bravery, and the rigid discipline which he maintained among the troops. Captain (now general) Champaigne,[21] who commanded the Royal Welch Fuzileers, also evinced the most perfect intrepidity and valor. Thus far I speak, not from the report of others, but from my own immediate observation.

The author cannot conclude the account of this day's victory, without entreating pardon from the reader, while he remarks that three years (excepting two months and a day) had elapsed since he was made prisoner at Saratoga by general Gates! He had at length, the satisfaction of seeing the same general to whom his majesty's forces, under Burgoyne surrendered, sustain a signal defeat. What were his feelings at that eventful moment! How did he bless that Providence which inspired him with the idea of effecting his escape, and preserved him to be a partaker of that triumph which the soldier feels, when his sovereign's troops are victorious over his enemies! More especially when that victory was obtained in the hard fought field over a general whose former success at Saratoga, had been trumpeted from one end of America to the other, and who had injured the British name, by charging the officers and privates with depredations that never existed but in his own imagination.

20. Francis, Lord Rawdon, commander of the Volunteers of Ireland, a loyalist regiment.
21. Forbes Champagne, captain in the 23rd Regiment of Foot.

CHAPTER NINE

[Campaign and Surrender, 1781]

Southern Campaign under Lord Cornwallis. General Greene succeeds Gates in the Command of the American Southern Army. Colonel Tarleton defeated at Cowpens. Lord Cornwallis crosses the Catawba. The Author's Narrative of that Transaction. Colonel Webster joins Lord Cornwallis. Lord Cornwallis retires from Hillsborough. Action of Guilford Court House. British Army arrives at Wilmington.

THE CAPTURE OF CHARLESTOWN, and the reduction of almost all the whole of South Carolina, naturally inclined the British commanders to extend their views to the conquest of North Carolina. I remember after the battle of Camden in marching through North Carolina I was ordered to cover the rear of our little army; one of my soldiers straggled away from the party and was shot. Stragglers are soon snapt; we are safest in a body.[1] The Americans on their part saw the necessity of reinforcing the southern army; and general Greene,[2] at the recommendation of Washington, was appointed to its command, which was transferred to him at Charlotte by general Gates. A country thinly inhabited, and abounding, with swamps, afforded every advantage to a partizan warfare over a large and regular

1. These two sentences are from the commonplace book.
2. Nathanael Greene, commander of the Continental army in the South.

army. This system was acted on by Greene, and accordingly general Morgan,[3] with a numerous detachment was directed to threaten the British post at Ninety Six, on the western extremity of South Carolina; the main body under general Greene at the same time, moving on to north side of Pedee, opposite Cheraw-Hill.

The British army, at that time, had marched two hundred miles from the sea-coast, and was preparing for an invasion of North Carolina. In order therefore to drive Morgan from its rear, and deter the inhabitants from joining his standard, lieutenant colonel Tarleton with six hundred men (three hundred of which were cavalry) proceeded against him. The engagement took place at Cowpens. The British, led on by the colonel himself, advanced, confident of victory, with a shout, and poured a tremendous fire on the enemy. The American line gave way, and fled; the British advanced, and engaged the second. At that critical moment, colonels Washington and Howard rallied the flying troops, and, joined by the militia, led them on to the support of the second line.[4] The British were thrown into confusion: three hundred were killed and wounded; the whole of the artillery-men (who worked the guns) that did not share their fate, were taken, with two three pounders, Colonel Tarleton, with about fifty of the cavalry, made a last, desperate, but glorious effort: he charged and repulsed Washington's horse, retook the baggage of the corps, cut the detachment who had it in possession to pieces, destroyed the greater part, and retired with the rest to Hamilton's Ford.*

This defeat (particularly the loss of the light infantry) was a severe loss to the royal camp. The prisoners were conveyed by forced

*In lord Cornwallis's dispatches to government concerning this engagement, he says, "In justice to the detachment of the royal artillery, I must here observe, that no terror could induce them to abandon their guns, and they were all killed and wounded in the defence of them."

3. Daniel Morgan, commander of the American forces at the battle of Cowpens in 1780.
4. William Washington and John Eager Howard, commanders of American regiments.

marches to Richmond; so that all attempts of the main army to recapture them were unavailing. The army halted during two days collecting provisions, and destroying superfluous baggage. Sometimes we had turnips served out for our food, when we came to a turnip field; or arriving at a field of corn, we converted our canteens into rasps and ground our Indian corn for bread; when we could get no Indian corn, we were compelled to eat liver as a substitute for bread, with our lean beef. In all this his lordship participated, nor did he indulge himself even in the distinction of a tent; but in all things partook our sufferings, and seemed much more to feel for us than for himself. We then marched through North Carolina, to the banks of the Dan, on the utmost extremities of the province.

It is a pleasing sight to see a column arrive at its halting ground.[5] The Camp is generally marked out, if circumstances allow of it, on the edge of some wood, and near a river or stream. The troops are halted in open columns and arms piled, pickets and guards paraded and posted, and in two minutes all appear at home. Some fetch large stones to form fire places; others hurry off with canteens and kettles for water while the wood resounds with the blows of the tomahawk. Dispersed under the more distant trees you see the officers, some dressing, some arranging a few boughs to shelter them by night, others kindling their own fires. How often under some spreading pine tree which afforded shade, shelter and fuel have I taken up my lodging for the night. Sitting in the midst of my comrades, men whom I loved and esteemed partaking of a coarse but wholesome meal, seasoned by hunger and cheefulness. Wrapt up in a blanket, the head reclining on a stone or a knapsack coved with the dews of the night or drenched perhaps by the thunder shower sleeps many a hardy veteran. A bivouack in heavy weather does not I allow present a very comfortable appearance. The officers sit shivering in their

5. This paragraph, with the title "The Bivouack of an Army," is from the commonplace book. Lamb did not specify whether it refers to Burgoyne's 1777 campaign or Cornwallis's 1781 campaign.

wet tents idle and angry. The men with their forage caps drawn over their ears huddle together under the trees or crowed round cheerless smoky fires—complaining of their commissaries, the rain and the Americans.

On the 1st day of February, at day light in the morning, we were directed to cross M'Cowan's Ford, in order to dislodge a party of the Americans under the command of General Davison,[6] which were strongly posted on the opposite hills. Lord Cornwallis, according to his usual manner, dashed first into the river, mounted on a very fine spirited horse, the brigade of guards[7] followed, two three pounders next, the Royal Welch Fuzileers after them. Colonel Webster had been previously directed to move with a strong guard division to Beattie's Ford, six miles above M'Cowan's in order to divide the attention of the Americans.

The place where we forded was about half a mile over.[8] The enemy stood on the hills of the opposite shore, which were high and steep, hanging over the river, so that they had every advantage over us, to facilitate their firing on those who attempted to cross there. Lord Cornwallis's fine horse was wounded under him, but his lordship escaped unhurt. Amidst these dreadful oppositions, we still urged through this rapid stream, striving with every effort to gain the opposite shore; just in the centre of the river, the bombardier[9] who was employed in steering one of the three pounders, unfortunately let go his hold of the helm of the gun, and being a low man, he was forced off his feet, and immediately carried headlong down the river. At that very instant, I was bringing up the division that covered this gun, and encouraging the men to hold fast by one another, and not to be dismayed at the enemy's fire, or from the rapidity or depth of the water, which was at this place more than

6. William Lee Davidson, an officer in a Continental regiment from North Carolina.
7. The Brigade of Guards, a corps composed of men detached from the three British regiments of foot guards in Great Britain.
8. "Half a mile over," the river was half a mile wide.
9. "Bombardier," a senior private soldier in the artillery.

four feet deep, and very rocky at the bottom. I knew that if this artillery man was either killed or drowned, his loss would be great indeed, as we had no man at hand that could supply his place in working the gun; this consideration darted through my mind in an instant, and I was determined to save his life or perish in the attempt. I therefore quitted my hold of the right hand man of my division, and threw myself on my belly on the surface of the water, and in nine or ten strong strokes, I overtook him. By this time he was almost exhausted, having been carried down the stream heels over head, upwards of forty yards. I got him on his feet, and led him back in safety to his gun. It was very remarkable, and taken particular notice of by the British troops, that during this transaction not one shot was fired at us by the Americans; indeed they might have easily shot us both in the head, as the current of the river carried us very near to them. After this affair the enemy began again a very heavy fire upon us, nevertheless our divisions waded on, in a cool intrepid manner, to return their fire, being impossible, as our cartouch boxes were all tied at the back of our necks. This urged us on with greater rapidity, till we gained the opposite shore, where we were obliged to scramble up a very high hill under, a heavy fire; several of our men were killed and wounded, before we reached the summit. The American soldiers did all that brave men could do, to oppose our passage across the river, and I believe not one of them moved from his post, till we mounted the hill, and used our bayonets; their general was the first man that received us sword in hand, and suffered himself to be cut to pieces sooner than retreat; after his death, his troops were soon defeated and dispersed. We fought with bayonets, a shower of blood rained from our weapons. Many a lifeless body fell to the earth; the buzzards of Carolina waded in the blood of the slain.[10]

Let the reader only for a moment consider what a situation the British troops were placed in, while they were wading over this ford,

10. This sentence is from the commonplace book.

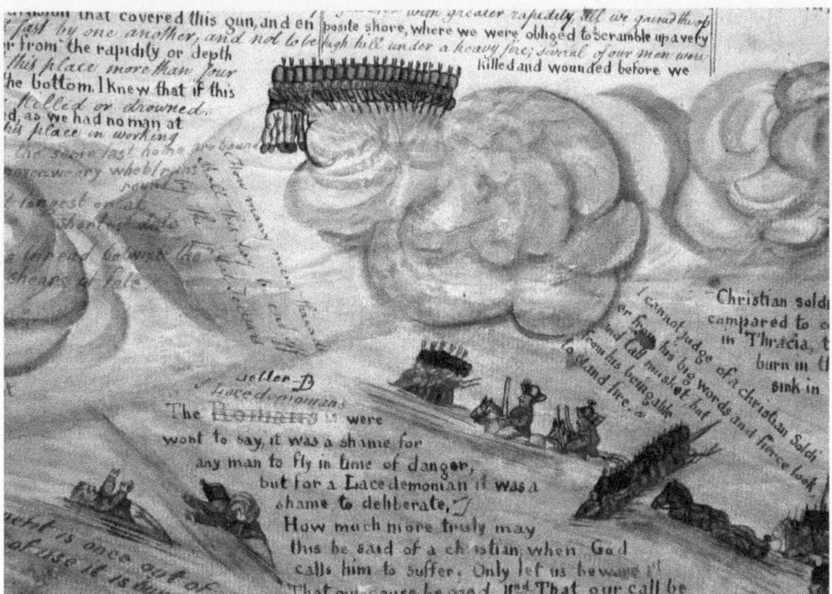

The illustration in Lamb's commonplace book of crossing the Catawba River, although stylized, primitive and depicting 1800s uniforms, accurately depicts wading through chest-deep water while under hostile fire. Methodist Historical Society of Ireland.

upwards of five hundred yards wide, up to their breast in a rapid stream, their knapsacks on their back, sixty or seventy rounds of powder and ball in each pouch, tied at the pole of their necks, their firelocks with bayonets, fixed on their shoulders, three hundred of their enemies (accounted the best marksmen in the world) placed on a hill as it were over their heads, keeping a continual and very heavy fire upon them.

Yet such was the resolution with which they encountered the danger and such the determined regularity which was observed, that only one officer, (lieutenant colonel Hall[11]) and three privates were killed, and thirty six wounded. A striking instance of what may be effected in situations, deemed by many as invincible impediments to the progress of an army, by coolness, courage, and resolution. It

11. Francis Hall, a captain in the Brigade of Guards.

may be necessary to mention, that lord Cornwallis's horse, though he was shot in the water, did not fall until he reached the shore. General Leslie's horses were carried down the river; and such was the rapidity of the stream, that brigadier general O'Hara's[12] horse rolled with him down the current, for near forty yards.

Lord Cornwallis's division having made good the dangerous passage of the Catawba, landed, and the 23d regiment, with the cavalry under colonel Tarleton, set out in pursuit of the militia. Intelligence being gained that the American militia had rendezvoused at Tarrant's Tavern, ten miles from Beattie's Ford, the 23d regiment halted half way, and the colonel proceeded with the cavalry alone. About five hundred were then prepared to receive him, who were immediately charged, their centre broken through, fifty killed and the rest dispersed. The gallantry of these actions made such an impression on the inhabitants, that the troops made their way without molestation to the Yadkin, notwithstanding the inveterate prejudice which this part of North Carolina bore to the British name. General Greene's plan of waiting till Huger and Williams joined him, was thus completely frustrated, the troops at the different fords were withdrawn, and Morgan began a precipitate retreat to the Yadkin.[13]

Meantime colonel Webster's division passed Beattie's Ford, on the Catawba, and joined that of lord Cornwallis on the road to Salisbury. They immediately began to pursue Morgan; but he reached the Trading Ford, and passed the Yadkin, with the loss of his baggage, which the flight of the riffle men left in possession of the king's troops. A heavy rain which fell during the night, rendered the fords impassible, and so swelled the river, that general Morgan having secured all the boats and flats on the opposite shore, the pursuit was rendered impossible, except by marching up the western banks of the Yadkin, and passing by the shallow fords near its source. This gave time for the junction of the American armies. In this situation,

12. Charles O'Hara, brigadier general and second in command to General Cornwallis.
13. American officers Isaac Huger and Otho Holland Williams.

it was the aim of lord Cornwallis to get between the American army and Virginia, and thereby cut off general Greene's retreat to that place. His lordship was, by some means, misled by false information relative to the lower fords being impassible, and began his march to the upper fords of the Dan. Of this, general Greene took advantage, and by a rapid flight, reached Boyd's and Irwine's Ferries, and passed the river; but so closely was he pursued by his lordship, that the last division had scarcely crossed, when the British reached the opposite banks. The difficulties and hardships which the troops endured in this ineffectual pursuit, were sustained with an heroism that was inspired by the idea of terminating the contest in this part by one decisive blow, which certainly would have been done, but for the mistake relative to the fords. General Greene having thus made his escape from North Carolina lord Cornwallis returned to Hillsborough, where he erected the royal standard, and issued a proclamation inviting all the loyal inhabitants to join him.

General Greene receiving intelligence of this, and dreading the consequences, took the daring measure of again crossing the Dan, with the legion of colonel Lee,[14] and returning to North Carolina.

Such was the scarcity of provisions at Hillsborough, that it was found impossible to support the army in that place. They were even obliged to kill some of their best draft horses. They therefore passed the Haw, and encamped in Allamance Creek. This movement much dispirited the loyalists, and raised the drooping hopes of the Americans. As the British retired, Greene advanced, crossed the Haw, and posted himself between Troublesome Creek and Reedy Fork, carefully changing his position every night, to avoid an engagement. In this situation, lord Cornwallis gave orders to beat up the American posts at Reedy Fork, in order to compel them to a greater distance, or perhaps allure Greene, who lay in the direction of Guildford Court-House, to a general engagement. Early in the

14. Henry Lee, commander of a corps of cavalry in the Continental army.

morning of the 6th of March, the army passed Allamance Creek, and marched towards Reedy Fork. The Americans were not unapprised of the movement, and hastily retreated across the Fork. General Greene instead of marching to their assistance, abandoned them to their fate. At Wedzell's Mill, they were overtaken by lieutenant colonel Webster, and numbers fell. The supplies and reinforcements which Greene anxiously expected, arrived at last, with the North Carolina militia, from the frontiers, making his numbers in the whole upwards of five thousand men.

Thus reinforced he determined to offer lord Cornwallis battle. He re-passed the Haw, and marched to Guildford Court-House, but twelve miles from the British army, at the Quakers' meeting house in the forks of Deep River.

On the 15th of March, about four miles from Guildford, the engagement began; colonel Tarleton led on the British advance. The Americans were commanded by general Lee,[15] who behaved with the most undaunted bravery, and maintained himself against the most formidable opposition, until the 23d regiment advancing to the support of Tarleton, compelled him to give way. Greene formed his order of battle on a commanding scite. It consisted of three lines. Two brigades of the North Carolina militia flanked by a wood, composed the first. That of Virginia formed the second. These were compleatly encompassed in the wood, three hundred yards in the rear of the first. Four hundred yards behind them, in open ground, near the Court House, the third was formed, consisting of two brigades of continental troops. Two corps of observation were placed on the right and left flanks; the one, commanded by colonel Washington, the other by colonel Lee. The British advance was formed by a column of royal artillery, under the command of lieutenant Macleod;[16] and the disposition of the main attack was as follows: the 71st, the regiment of Bose, commanded by general Leslie, and

15. Henry Lee, who was a lieutenant colonel.
16. John McLeod of the Royal Artillery.

the 1st battalion of guards, colonel Norton,[17] formed the right line; the 23d and 33d led on by colonel Webster, and supported by brigadier general O'Hara, and the grenadiers and 2d battalion of guards, constituted the left; corps of observation, light infantry of the guards, and yagers, on the left of the artillery, and the cavalry in column behind on the road.

These masterly dispositions preluded one of the most signal battles ever gained by British valour. This day we fought with men, for some days before we were fighting with hunger.[18] The details are so accurately laid down by Stedman,[19] who had every opportunity of ascertaining even the minutest circumstances that it may be better to quote his account of it, than by aiming at originality, fall short of the particulars. "This disposition being made, the line received orders to advance, and moved forward with that steady and guarded, but firm and determined resolution whcih discipline alone can confer. It has been remarked by an eye-witness* that "the order and coolness of that part of Webster's brigade which advanced across the open ground, exposed to the enemy's fire, could not be sufficiently extolled." At the distance of one hundred and forty yards they received the enemy's first fire, but continued to advance unmoved. When arrived at a nearer and more convenient distance, they delivered their own fire, and rapidly charged with their bayonets: the enemy did not wait the shock, but retreated behind their second line. In other parts of the line the British troops behaved with equal gallantry, and were not less successful. The second line of the enemy made a braver and stouter resistance than the first. Posted in the woods, and covering themselves with trees, they kept up for a considerable time a galling fire, which did great execution.

*Lieutenant colonel Tarleton.

17. Chapel Norton, a captain in the Brigade of Guards.
18. This sentence is from the commonplace book.
19. Charles Stedman, *The History of the Origin, Progress, and Termination of the American War* (London: Printed for the Author, 1794).

At length, however, they were compelled to retreat, and fall back upon the continentals. In this severe conflict the whole of the British infantry were engaged. General Leslie, from the great extent of the enemy's front, reaching far beyond his right, had been very early obliged to bring forward the 1st battalion of the guards, appointed for his reserve, and form it into line: and lieutenant colonel Webster, finding the left of the 33d regiment exposed to a heavy fire from the right wing of the enemy, which greatly out-flanked him, changed its front to the left, and the ground become vacant by this movement, was immediately occupied by general O'Hara, with the grenadiers, and 2d battalion of the guards. Webster moving to the left with the 33d regiment, supported by the light infantry of the guards, and the yagers, routed and put to flight the right wing of the enemy, and in his progress, after two severe struggles, gained the right of the continentals; but the superiority of their numbers, and the weight of their fire obliged him, separated as he was from the British line, to re-cross a ravine, and occupy an advantageous position on the opposite bank, until he could hear of the progress of the king's troops on the right. The British line being so much extended to the right and left, in order to shew a front equal to the enemy, was unavoidably broken into intervals in the pursuit of the first and second American lines; some parts of it being more advanced than others, in consequence of the different degrees of resistance that had been met with, or of other impediments arising from the thickness of the woods, and the inequality of the ground. The whole however, moved forward; and the second battalion of the guards, commanded by the honorable colonel Stuart,[20] was the first that reached the open ground at Guildford Court House. Impatient to signalize themselves, they immediately attacked a body of continentals, greatly superior in numbers, that was seen formed on the left of the road, routed them and took their cannon, being two six-pounders; but pursuing them with too much ardour and im-

20. James Stewart, a captain in the Brigade of Guards.

petuosity towards the wood on their rear, were thrown into confusion by a heavy fire received from a body of continentals, who were yet unbroken, and being instantly charged by Washington's dragoons, were driven back with great slaughter, and the loss of the cannon that had been taken. Lieutenant Macleod, advancing, along the road with the royal artillery, had by this time reached the open ground. By a spirited and well-directed cannonade he checked the pursuit of the Americans. Fortunately also, the 71st regiment, belonging to general Leslie's division, was seen emerging from the woods on the right, and the 23d not long afterwards, made its appearance on the left. To the right and left of these regiments, general O'Hara, although severely wounded, rallied with much gallantry and great expedition, the remains of the 2d battalion of the guards; and the Americans were quickly repulsed and put to flight, with once more the loss of the two six-pounders: two other six-pounders were also taken, being all the artillery which they had in the field, and two ammunition waggons. The 71st pushed forward to an eminence at the Court House, on the left flank of the continentals. Lieutenant colonel Webster again advanced across the ravine, defeated the corps that was opposed to him, and connected himself with the centre of the British line. The continentals of the American army being now driven from their ground, as well as the militia, a general retreat took place; but it was conducted with order and regularity. The 23d and 71st, with part of the cavalry, were at first sent in pursuit of the enemy, but afterwards received orders to return. It is probable that, as the British commander became more acquainted with all circumstances of the action, and the number of the killed and wounded, he found it necessary to countermand his orders, and desist from the pursuit. The action being now ended in the centre and left of the British line, a firing was still heard on the right, where general Leslie with the 1st battalion of the guards and the regiment of Bose, had been greatly impeded in advancing, by the excessive thickness of the woods, which rendered their bayonets of little use. The broken corps of the enemy were thereby encouraged to make frequent stands, and to throw in an irregular fire; so that this part of the British line was at times warmly engaged in front, flank, and rear, with some of the enemy that had been routed in the first attack, and with part of the extremity of their left wing, which, by the closeness of the woods, had been passed unseen.

"At one period of the action the first battalion of the guards was completely broken. It had suffered greatly in ascending a woody height to attack the second line of the Americans, strongly posted upon the top of it, who, availing themselves of the advantages of their situation, retired, as soon as they had discharged their pieces, behind the brow of the hill, which protected them from the shot of the guards, and returned as soon as they had loaded, and were again in readiness to fire. Notwithstanding the disadvantage under which the attack was made, the guards reached the summit of the eminence, and put this part of the American line to flight: but no sooner was it done, than another line of the Americans presented itself to view, extending far beyond the right of the guards, and inclining towards their flank, so as almost to encompass them. The ranks of the guards had been thinned in ascending the height, and a number of the officers had fallen: captain Maitland,[21] who at this time received a wound, retired to the rear, and having had his wound dressed, returned immediately to join the battalion of guards to which he belonged. Some of the men, too, from superior exertions, had reached the summit of the eminence sooner than others; so that the battalion was not in regular order when it received the fire of the third American line. The enemy's fire being repeated and continued, and, from the great extent of their line, being poured in not only on the front but flank of the battalion, completed its confusion and disorder, and notwithstanding every exertion made by the remaining officers, it was at last entirely broken. Fortunately, at this time, the Hessian regiment of Bose, commanded by lieutenant colonel de Bury,[22]

21. Augustus Maitland, a captain in the Brigade of Guards.

22. Johann Christian du Buy, lieutenant colonel commanding the Regiment von Bose.

which had hitherto suffered but little, was advancing in firm and compact order on the left of the guards, to attack the enemy. Lieutenant colonel Norton thought the fortunate arrival of the regiment of Bose presented a favorable opportunity for forming again his battalion, and requested the Hessian lieutenant-colonel to wheel his regiment to the right, and cover the guards, whilst their officers endeavoured to rally them. The request was immediately and most gallantly complied with; and, under the cover of the fire of the Hessians, the exertions of lieutenant colonel Norton, and his few remaining officers, were at last successful in restoring order. The battalion, being again formed, instantly moved forward to join the Hessians: the attack was renewed, and the enemy were defeated. But here the labours of this part of the line did not yet cease. No sooner had the guards and Hessians defeated the enemy in front, than they found it necessary to return and attack another body of them that appeared in the rear; and in this manner they were obliged to traverse the same ground in various directions, before the enemy were completely put to the rout. The firing heard on the right, after the termination of the action in the centre, and on the left, induced lord Cornwallis to detach Tarleton, with part of the cavalry, to gain intelligence of what was doing in that quarter, and to know whether general Leslie wanted assistance. But before Tarleton's arrival on the right, the affair was over, and the British troops were standing with ordered arms;[23] all resistance having ceased on the part of the Americans, except from a few hardy riflemen, who lurking behind trees, occasionally fired their pieces, but at such a distance as to do no mischief. These colonel Tarleton, when requested, readily undertook to disperse with his cavalry, and rushing forward under cover of a general volley of musquetry from the guards and the regiment of Bose, quickly performed what was expected of him. In this affair colonel Tarleton himself received a slight wound, but the rest of his corps returned unhurt."

23. "Ordered arms," a position with the firelock by the right side with the butt on the ground.

As the Author belonged to colonel Webster's brigade, he is enabled, (and the Reader will naturally expect it from him,) to state some circumstances unnoticed by any historian, from his own personal observation. After the brigade formed across the open ground, the colonel rode on to the front, and gave the word, *"Charge."* Instantly the movement was made, in excellent order, in a smart run, with arms charged: when arrived within forty yards of the enemy's line, it was perceived that their whole force had their arms presented, and resting on a rail fence, the common partitions in America. They were taking aim with the nicest precision.

"Twixt host and host but narrow space was left,
"A *dreadful* interval, and, front to front,
"Presented, stood in terrible array."[24]

At this awful period a general pause took place; both parties surveyed each other for the moment with the most anxious suspense. Nothing speaks, *the general* more than seizing on decisive moments: colonel Webster rode forward in the front of the 23d regiment, and said, with more than even his usual commanding voice (which was well known to his Brigade,) *"Come on, my brave Fuzileers."* This operated like an inspiring voice, they rushed forward amidst the enemy's fire; dreadful was the havoc on both sides.

"Amazing scene!
What showers of mortal hail! What flaky fires!"[25]

At last the Americans gave way, and the brigade advanced, to the attack of their second line. Here the conflict became still more fierce. Before it was completely routed, where I stood, (it is not from egotism, but to be the better understood, that I here, without breaking the thread of precision, assume the first person) I observed an American officer attempting to fly. I immediately darted after him, but he perceiving my intention to capture him, fled with the utmost speed. I pursued, and was gaining on him, when, hearing a confused noise on my left, I observed several bodies of Americans drawn up

24. From John Milton, *Paradise Lost*, 1667.
25. From Watts, *The celebrated Victory*, 1706.

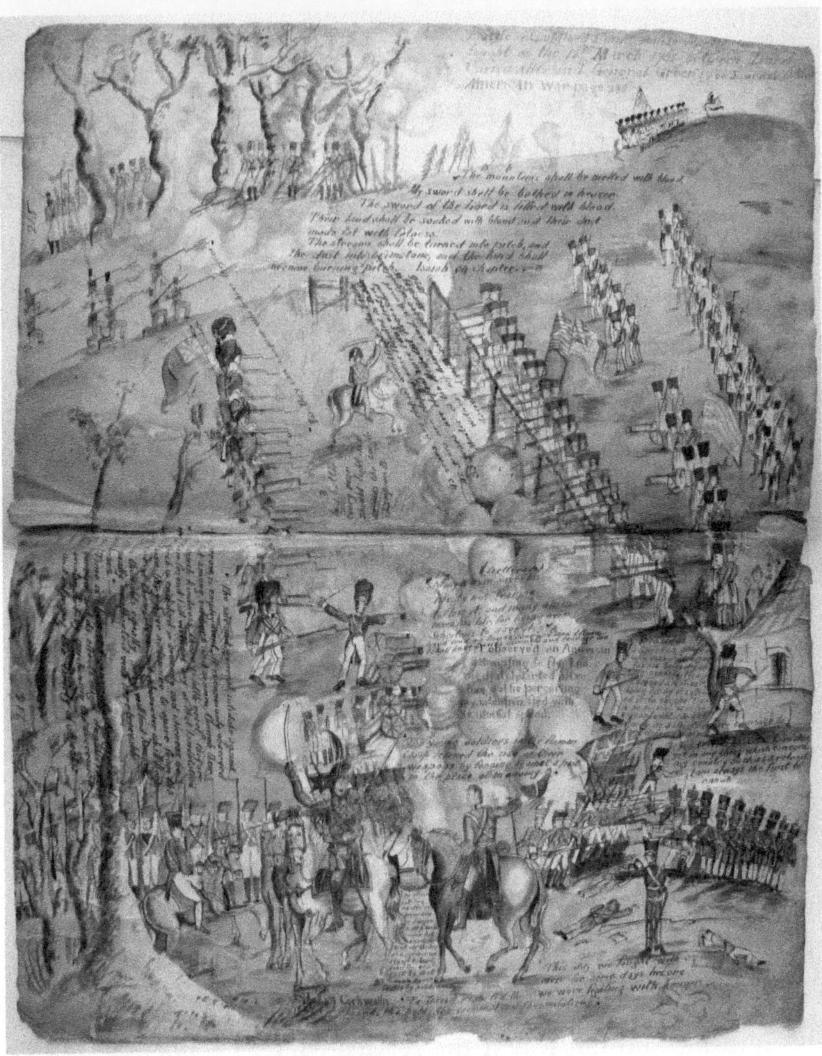

The two-page illustration in Lamb's commonplace book of the Battle of Guildford Courthouse is not stylistically accurate but does capture the complexity and confusion of this running battle. Methodist Historical Society of Ireland.

within the distance of a few yards. Whoever has been in an engagement well knows that, in such moments all fears of death are over. Seeing one of the guards among the slain,[26] where I stood, I stopped

26. "One of the guards," a soldier of the Brigade of Guards.

and replenished my own pouch with the cartridges that remained in his; during the time I was thus employed, several shots were fired at me; but not one took effect. Glancing my eye the other way, I saw a company of the guards advancing to attack these parties. The Reader may perhaps be surprised at the bravery of troops, thus with calm intrepidity attacking superior numbers, when formed into separate bodies, and all acting together; but I can assure him this instance was not peculiar; it frequently occurred in the British army, during the American war. It was impossible to join this company, as several of the American parties lay between me and it. I had no time for deliberation. How to act I knew not. On the instant, however, I saw lord Cornwallis riding across the clear ground. His lordship was mounted on a dragoon's horse (his own having been shot;) the saddle-bags were under the creature's belly, which much retarded his progress, owing to the vast quantity of underwood that was spread over the ground; his lordship was evidently unconscious of his danger. I immediately laid hold of the bridle of his horse, and turned his head. I then mentioned to him, that if his lordship had pursued the same direction, he would in a few moments have been surrounded by the enemy, and, perhaps, cut to pieces or captured. I continued to run along side of the horse, keeping the bridle in my hand, until his lordship, gained the 23d regiment, which was at that time drawn up in the skirt of the woods.

To the honor of lord Cornwallis, it should be mentioned, that his lordship did not forget the service which I rendered him. On March 22, a few days after the battle of Guildford Court House, I was ordered to mount guard over the prisoners which we had taken at that battle.[27] Among them was an American captain who had committed various depredations on the loyal inhabitants of the country.

This man was particularly mentioned to me, by the provost marshal. I was ordered to be very careful that he should not make his

27. The date is given in the commonplace book.

escape, for lord Cornwallis was apprehensive he might murder and destroy the inhabitants, whom he knew had assisted us in our march. Unfortunately, he bribed one of my sentries, who permitted him to effect it. When the circumstance was made known to his lordship he was highly displeased, and command the serjeant of the guard to be brought before him, in order to be confined. But when I was approaching towards him, his countenance changed into a smile, and he directed his aid-de-camp to tell me to go to my regiment, and to confine the sentinel who had permitted the captain to get out of confinement. Mild language is worth much and costs little. If this favour from lord Cornwallis was less than looked for yet it was more than I deserved. Lord Cornwallis in reproving Serjeant Lamb concealed the lancet of reproof in the sponge of insinuating and affectionate address—Let great men go and do likewise to their inferiors. I do not murmur nor complain because his lordship did not take me under his protection and become my patron (I never had a patron in this world).[28]

General Greene fled to Reedy Fork Creek, where, when he had passed the river, he halted on the opposite banks to collect his stragglers. When he had partly accomplished this, he pushed on to Troublesome Creek, about twelve miles further. Lord Cornwallis, (from the army being in want of provisions, and its several other distresses,) found it would be inadvisable to pursue the fugitives. It on the other hand became indispensably necessary to move towards some place where supplies might be obtained. Accordingly about seventy wounded were left at the Quaker's meeting house, under protection of a flag of truce, and the army slowly retired to Cross Creek.

It was part of lord Cornwallis's plan for the operation in the north, that colonel Balfour, the commandant at Charlestown, should dispatch a force by water, sufficient to take Wilmington, as a post of communication, and a medium of obtaining supplies. This

28. These sentences, from "Mild language," are from the commonplace book.

service was executed by major Craig in the end of January, and put in a proper state of defence, Wilmington lies near the mouth of Cape Fear River; and Cross Creek (a settlement of loyal Highlanders) is on a branch of it, about one hundred miles up the country. From thence it was expected the army would obtain supplies, and it was moreover admirably adapted, from its central situation, as a rallying point for those who were well affected to the royal cause. Lord Cornwallis began his march from Guildford Court House by issuing a proclamation, inviting the loyal to his standard, and offering pardon to those who should return to their allegiance. His lordship then proceeded by slow marches to Cross Creek; general Greene following him as far as Ramsey's Mill, on Deep River. Nothing but slight occasional skirmishes ensued during the march. On his arrrival at the Creek, every hope was disappointed. Four days forage could not be had in twenty miles, all communication, with Wilmington from the narrowness of the river, was impracticable, and the scattered inhabitants on its lofty banks were irreconcilably hostile. The troops therefore began their march to Wilmington, at which place they arrived on the 7th of April. During these toilsome movements, the British army sustained an almost irreparable loss, by the deaths of colonel Webster of the 33d, captains Schutz and Maynard of the guards, and captain Wilmouski and ensign De Trott of the regiment of Bose. They all received their mortal wounds at Guildford Court House.*

It was the intention of lord Cornwallis to have moved on to Camden, to obtain supplies, and messengers were accordingly dispatched to lord Rawdon, but unhappily they never reached his lordship. The intelligence that Greene had marched to attack lord Rawdon, and that probably the fate of Camden was already decided, inclined his lordship to pursue a different direction, and the army set out for Virginia.

*It was reported in the army, that when lord Cornwallis received the news of colonel Webster's death, his lordship was struck with such pungent sorrow, that turning himself, he looked on his sword, and emphatically exclaimed, "I have lost my scabbard."

On the 22d of September, 1781, our army arrived at York-town in the state of Virginia. At this conjuncture, the Colonial force, aided by the French under Count Rochambeau, amounted to nineteen thousand effective men, who followed to make an attack on us in our lines. Notwithstanding the very great superiority, (the British army consisting of not more than Five thousand fighting men) they did not immediately attack, although Lord Cornwallis was prepared to give battle.

On the 30th of September the Siege commenced, and not until the 6th of October did the enemy finish his first paralel covering our whole left flank, distant about six hundred yards. On the 9th in the evening their batteries opened.

On the night of the 11th, the enemy began their second paralel, nearer to us by three hundred yards, and after making several severe attempts on the evening of the 14th, they assaulted and carried two redoubts, which had been advanced to retard their approaches and to cover our left. In this state of things, reduced in force and disabled to withstand his adversaries, Lord Cornwallis thought it would be a wanton sacrifice of his brave little army to continue the conflict, and therefore, with the advice of his officers, he resolved to capitulate. Previous to the taking of the redoubts our army by sickness and actual losses of men in the enemy's attacks, and in sorties, suffered so much that Lord Cornwallis's prospect of attaining any object by fighting, particularly when the redoubts were taken, was hopeless in the extreme. The enemy made great sacrifices to aggravate the evils of the extremity in which they pressed on us, and for this purpose, an emulation was raised between the French and Americans by leading them to the attack separately, to excite extraordinary exertions.

The Royal Welch Fuzileers were greatly exposed to the fire of a battery of nine guns which neared us about the distance of 50, or 60 yards. At the commencement of the campaign this regiment was 500 strong, but then it was reduced to about 120, who had to maintain their post on this galling occasion, as they did with great gallantry, until we were entirely exhausted, and the Writer of this Memoir was so worn out that he could no longer stand, and was at length relieved by a non-commissioned officer, who, in a few minutes after, fell by a ball sent from a nine pounder. The Author of course considered his being taken away from his post by excess of fatigue as an interposition of that providence which shielded him from instant dissolution frequently before.

The garrison was reduced to the last extremity, not a gun remained on that part of the works attacked by the enemy, scarcely a shell was left, the works in tumbling to ruin not a gun could be fired from them, and only one eight inch, and a little more than 100 cohorn shells remained. They were in many places assailable already, and if the fire continued a few hours longer it would be madness to attempt to maintain them with the present garrison (4017 fit for duty) exhausted by the fatigue of constant watching and unremitting duty encompassed a bout with a mighty host of the picked troops of France and America, aided by a formidable navy, and to sum up our difficulties, we were attacked by famine in our camp. On the 19th October 1781 the posts of York and Gloucester were surrendered to general Washington as commander in chief of the combined army, and the ships of war, transports, and other vessels to the Count dc Grasse, as commander of the French fleet. The combined army consisted of 7000 French and nearly the same number of continental soldiers, and about 5000 militia. Thirty sail of the line of battle ships manned with 25000 seamen, half of whom might act on shore. This defeat did not tarnish the fame of the British arms when it is considered that our troops had boldy marched through the heart of the enemies country. It was never said of Burgoyne's army that they ran away, but that they were slain. Nor of Cornwallis' army that they were vanquished but that they were taken.[29]

29. This paragraph is from the commonplace book.

CHAPTER TEN

[Second Escape to New York]

Escapes from Yorktown. Traverses the Woods. Re-taken at Frederick-town. Attempts to escape, but is detected. Confined in Jail. Marched Prisoner to Winchester. Marched to Little York. Escapes with a small Party. Arrives at Staten Island, and at last effects his escape to New York.

IN CONSEQUENCE OF THIS disastrous capitulation, the Author became a second time a prisoner of the Americans. Fortunately for him, he was not recognized as one who had formerly made his escape, but ordered to march with the rest of the British troops to Winchester, situate in the back parts of Virginia, upwards of two hundred miles distant from York Town. In this part of his Journal (which, in absence of a better phrase, he almost ventures to call an historical episode) as in the narrative of his escape, after being made prisoner at Saratoga, and for the same reasons, he takes the liberty of conveying what befel him to the Reader's attention in the first person.

ESCAPE FROM YORK TOWN.

After the army under lord Cornwallis became prisoners, I was attached to the general hospital. I had frequently officiated as an assistant surgeon, both in the 9th and 23d regiments; and sometimes, when we had not a professional surgeon, I had endeavored, to do that duty, to the best of my knowledge. The great fatigue which I underwent during the siege, brought on a severe illness, from which having somewhat recovered, I determined to attempt my escape to New York, (the distance from York Town to New York is upwards of five hundred miles.) I accordingly waited on the surgeon general, and resigned my situation in the general hospital, acquainting him that I intended to follow the troops to Winchester. Having received the balance due to me,[1] I changed my dress, and appeared as a private soldier. The next consideration was, how to elude the French and American sentinels who guarded the prisoners. This I fortunately accomplished on November 28, 1781 while the guards were relieving,[2] and got outside of the two barriers, on the great road which led to Frederick-town in Maryland. I immediately struck into the woods, to avoid the picquet guard, which I knew was posted on it. Night approaching, and finding myself very weak, I made every exertion to extricate myself from the wood. Before it was completely dark, I perceived a few houses, and went into one of them. I entreated the inhabitants to let me remain there all night; this they refused in the most peremptory terms, and immediately turned me out of doors, threatening, that if I did not instantly depart, they would take me back a prisoner to Gloucester Point. I went away with a very sorrowful heart, and after remaining some time in the woods, scarcely able to determine what course to take, the weather being very severe and cold, and finding myself becoming very weak, I made a desperate effort, and went into a house, where there was a woman surrounded by a number of children. I asked her the favor of remaining in her house for the night. She looked at me very sternly, and said, "How can you expect such a favor from me, or any of the Americans, seeing you came from England with an intent to destroy our country?" As I stood talking with her, her husband came in. He seemed to be a humane man, and said, "It would be very hard indeed to turn you out of my door such a severe evening as this. I

1. "The balance due to me," the pay owed to him for his work in the hospital.
2. The date is given in the commonplace book.

will permit you to remain here this night." He then desired his wife to get a little straw, and make me a bed near the fire place. After supper I Lay down; and not being disturbed by the roaring of cannon, and the alarm of war, which had been my portion for months before, I slept soundly, and awaked in the morning greatly refreshed. I gave the children some trifling presents, with which they and their parents seemed much gratified, and left them with the warmest emotions of thankfulness.

During this day (the 29th of November) I marched very hard on the main road, without encountering any interruption, this arose from its being the route which our troops had taken, the inhabitants thinking that I had not been able to keep up with the party, had lagged behind, and was endeavouring to overtake them. In the evening I came to a large building, when a gentleman accosted me, observing; "there are a great many of your men in this house, who are determined to remain in the country, they have hired themselves to different gentlemen. You had better join with them: you shall be well used, and in a short time you may become a citizen of America." Upon my entering the house, I found that there were above forty British soldiers, who had hired themselves to different gentlemen about the country. Early on the next morning, their masters came with horses, &c. and took them away. I was strongly importuned to go with them; but my mind revolted at the thought. When I was preparing to leave the house, the gentleman said to me, "You had better remain with me. I am told you can write a good hand, and understand accounts; I will build a school-house for you, and make you as comfortable as I can." I felt my whole frame agitated at the proposal, and notwithstanding the weather was stormy and severe, and that I was very unwell, I immediately left his house with indignation. This dishonorable practice of enticing the British soldiers to become settlers, was but too common, during the greater part of the American war. When a prisoner with them, I was often strongly solicited, and promised many rewards, if I would desert, and remain in the country. At one time I refused the acceptance of a debenture of land, amounting to 300 Acres, in Kentucky which then attracted a number of emigrants, in consequence of its being explored and settled by Daniel Boone, who published inviting accounts of the soil and climate. But I was determined to die rather than serve any state hostile to Great Britain: indeed I could not even patiently support the idea of remaining a prisoner among them. I had not travelled many miles when I overtook a serjeant of the 71st, and a drummer of the 23d. I immediately began persuading them to venture with me in attempting to escape. They both consented. How entwined about the very heart of man, is the love of liberty! From that source more than the soundness of my arguments, or the probability of realizing them, I prevailed. It is very easy to talk about going through a tract of land, five or six hundred miles covered with enemies; but when entangled in the wood, sinking in the swamp, or fording the rapid torrent, we find it an enterprise of much difficulty and danger.

However we addressed ourselves to our journey with confidence; but the next day our drummer complained that we marched too hard for him, and that it was impossible for us ever "to make good our escape. And (said he) for my part, I will stay where I am, and solace myself after all my hardships." No arguments which we could urge, appearing sufficient to cure his despondency, or alter his determination, we left him, and proceeded on our journey. The next day we overtook a waggon which was going to Philadelphia. By a short conversation, we soon discovered that the waggoner was a loyalist, and in consequence informed him, that we were making our escape to New York. He proposed to conceal us in his waggon as far as Philadelphia at which place his master lived. This was gladly received on our part, and we promised him an adequate reward; we proceeded with him in high spirits: but, unfortunately for us, we overtook an American soldier, who insisted on his being taken into the waggon. This disconcerted our plan for the present. We were fast approaching Frederick-town, through which we could not pass concealed in the waggon, on account of the presence of the American soldier: we therefore thought it far more prudent to quit the waggon entirely, and boldly march through the town on foot. The faithful waggoner, before he left us, promised to wait a few miles on the other side of the town, until we should rejoin him. But how vain are all human schemes! Soon as the waggon entered the town, the American gave the alarm, and a party of soldiers was ordered out to apprehend us. We were seized and brought through the town, in triumph. Many British soldiers were prisoners in this town, and among them the regiment to which my companion belonged.[3] We were huddled among them. Indeed our place of confinement was a most deplorable situation. Forty or fifty British soldiers crowded together in a small room. It is true we had a large parade to walk about in the day; but as the winter was remarkably cold, very few availed themselves of that privilege.

I examined this place of confinement minutely, and soon discovered, that it was surrounded by a chain of American sentinels. I likewise gained information, that small parties of the prisoners (under a strong guard) were often ordered out to get wood for firing.[4] It immediately occurred to me that the only chance for my escape, lay in getting myself enrolled in one of these wood cutting parties. I soon obtained this favor, and immediately began to take my measures: I strove to persuade as many of the party as I could to venture an escape with me. All my arguments proved ineffectual, except with one man, and my old companion the serjeant. I waited with anxious suspense for the moment we were to be called out to wood cutting. I emptied my knapsack, and distributed my superfluous necessaries, putting on three shirts, and taking an additional pair of shoes in my pocket. With my blanket wrapped about my shoulders, I sallied out when the call came, bearing my hatchet: the intended companions of my flight were privately directed to keep as near to me as possible. When we had arrived at the wood, about half a mile

3. The 71st Regiment was among those captured at Yorktown.
4. "Firing," fire wood.

from the place of confinement, we set to the work of cutting. I observed to one of our guards, that I saw a fine large maple tree a few yards beyond him; and begged permission for me and my two companions to cut it down. With that rudeness which ever characterizes the low mind when in office, he, in a surly manner, acquiesced in the proposal, little dreaming that we all intended to give him the slip. The better to color our pretence, and to cover our escape, we immediately set about cutting down the tree, keeping our eyes constantly fixed on the guard. At last he turned himself about, to watch the other prisoners. We seized the opportunity, and darted into the thickest part of the wood. Fear and hope (being pretty nearly balanced in our minds,) were the wings which urged our flight. I could run fast at this time. I held nothing to retard my flight. I had more brains than sovereigns or bank notes.[5] Our guards must have possessed the feet of deer before they could possibly have overtaken us. We ran on through the woods, as near as I could conjecture, during two hours, scarcely stopping to take breath. At last we arrived at a deep and rapid river. Fortunately for us, we soon discovered a ferry-boat, and on paying the fare, we crossed, without being examined, and pursued our way through the woods.

It should have been mentioned, that though we had on our regimentals,[6] we disguised ourselves by wrapping our blankets about us, which rather gave us the appearance of Indians than of British soldiers. We had not, however, proceeded far, when we were met by an armed party of Americans, who instantly surrounded us, and brought us back prisoners to the town. The serjeant, my companion, was then separated from me, as his regiment were prisoners near the town; he was turned in along with them, while I was sent a prisoner to their guard-house, where I was used in the most cruel manner. The American soldiers of Frederick Town had Tigers hearts. They were fierce without provocation, and cruel without necessity.

5. These three sentences are from the commonplace book.
6. "Regimentals," uniforms of their regiments.

This page of Lamb's commonplace book depicts three aspects of his confinement in Frederick Town, Maryland. At left, "In this guard house serjeant Lamb received cruel usage"; lower center, "Serjeant Lamb marched prisoner from the guard house to the town,"; and at right, "Town Goal," "Here, Serjeant Lamb was in a hotter furnace than in the guard house." Methodist Historical Society of Ireland.

This I experienced in their guard house.[7] The weather was extremely cold, (the latter end of November,) the guard-house was an open block-house, through which the snow and frost made their way in every direction. I procured, with much trouble, a little straw to lie upon, in one corner. But I soon found that my lodging would be a very hard one; for when the guard used to discover that I had fallen asleep, they applied a firebrand to the straw, and as it blazed, they set up a yell like the Indians, rejoicing in my distress, and deriding my endeavours to extinguish the flames. These savages felt as little by sorrow at my distress, as the under taker though dressed in black, feels sorry at a funeral.[8] When the relief used to be turned out, I sometimes took the liberty of drawing near the fire, to warm my

7. These three sentences are from the commonplace book.
8. This sentence is from the commonplace book.

half frozen limbs, but this indulgence was of short duration, for when the sentinels were relieved they came pouring into the guard-house, and, if found near the fire, I was usually buffetted about from one to the other, and perhaps a dozen fixed bayonets at once placed at my breast. When I found that I could obtain no mercy from these savages, and that every day I was worse used than on the preceding; I wrote a letter to the American commanding officer, informing him of the cruel usage which I daily received, and entreating him to permit me to be confined in the town goal. This request was at last granted; but my condition was not bettered by it. There I was confined in the upper part of the prison, which I had to ascend by a long board, which was almost perpendicular. In this dreary situation, without any fire-place, were twelve criminals. These men received a very small allowance of provisions; but, as for my part, not a morsel was alloted me. My poor fellow prisoners took compassion, and shared their pittance with me. Had it not been for their compassion, I should have been starved to death.

As for the jail I know it right well, it was a house of misery to me.[9] I remained in this place during twelve days, suffering the bitings of hunger by day, and shivering all night with the cold. It can scarcely be imagined that aught could possibly have added to my sufferings: yet was the case worse, for we were continually annoyed with the yellings of a black woman, who was confined for the murder of her child at the bottom of the jail. She used to yell the whole night long. Here, Serjeant Lamb was in a hotter furnace than in the guard house. In this house of misery serjeant Lamb's locks were well blazed and his bones crackled in this furnace.[10]

The reason of the bad usage which I in particular received, originated, it is most probable, in two distinct causes. This town had suffered much by the deaths of several young men, who had been killed during the war: the regiment of horse which was cut to pieces

9. This sentence is from the commonplace book.
10. This sentence is from the commonplace book.

at Long Island was composed almost entirely of the inhabitants of this part of the country. This was a source of general inveteracy to all British prisoners. I had every mischief arising from this cause to support in common with my fellow prisoners. But what rendered me still further an object of their particular severity was, their firm conviction that I still meditated my escape. This principally, if not entirely rose, I believe, from one of Burgoyne's army, who had deserted from his regiment, and was then in town. This man certainly informed the Americans that I had made my escape from that army into New York, and that I would do so again if I was not well taken care of. One might imagine that I might as well attempt to stop a torrent with my finger as to break away from these savages.[11] However, I was determined, if possible to extricate myself from my present dreadful situation. With that intent I wrote a letter to major Gordon[12] of the 80th regiment, who was then prisoner in the town, letting him know my distressed situation, and entreating his intercession with the American commander, to obtain my liberation from jail, and my being placed with the rest of my comrades, in their confinement near the town. The major was not unmindful of me; for although he was at that time laboring under a complication of disorders, arising from the excessive fatigue he had undergone during the siege, and the sufferings of his confinement, he referred my case to captain Coote of the 33d regiment, (now lieutenant-general Sir Eyre Coote[13]) with his desire that application might he made to the American commanders for the privilege which I desired: Captain Coote most humanely interceded for me, and obtained my request.

While the faculties of my nature remain entire, I never can forget the affecting interview which took place between the captain and me. A guard was ordered to conduct me from the jail to his quarters.

11. This sentence is from the commonplace book.
12. James Gordon, major in the 80th Regiment of Foot.
13. Eyre Coote, a captain in the 37th Regiment of Foot (not the 33rd as Lamb wrote).

While I was relating to him the sufferings which I had undergone since my being captured at York Town, and my determination and hope still to effect my escape into New York, the tear of sympathy filled his eyes, he condoled with me in our common lot, and encouraged me to persevere. He then directed the serjeants of the 33d regiment to build me a hut upon the ground where they were confined, and to take me into their mess. He gave me a guinea,[14] and I went off to my companions in triumph.

But my joy was only of short duration. Scarcely was I settled in my hut (in some degree of ease and comfort, in comparison to my former sufferings,) when I was ordered to be moved under a guard to Winchester, where the regiment to which I belonged was confined. The officers and men were all glad to see me: they had heard of the hardships I had endured in attempting my escape, and they condoled with me: part of the British troops remained here until January 1782, when congress ordered us to be marched to Little York, in Pennsylvania. I received information, that as soon as I fell into the ranks to march off, I should be taken and confined in Winchester jail, as the Americans were apprehensive, that when I got near to New York I should again attempt my escape to that place, I was advised by my officers to conceal myself until the troops had marched. I took the hint and hid myself in the hospital among the sick, here I remained until the American guards had been two days on their march with the British prisoners. I then prepared to follow them, but at a cautious distance. The troops arrived at Little York, and were confined in a prison similar to that which I have already described at Rutland, only a little more limited. About two hundred yards from this penn, a small village had been built by the remains of general Burgoyne's army, who were allowed very great privileges with respect to their liberty in the country. When some of my former comrades of the 9th regiment, were informed that I was a prisoner in lord Cornwallis's army, and that I was shortly expected at

14. "Guinea," a gold coin worth twenty-one shillings.

Little York, they immediately applied to the commanding officer of the Americans for a pass in my name, claiming me as one of their regiment. This was immediately granted, and some of them kindly and attentively placed themselves on the watch for my arrival, lest I should be confined with the rest of lord Cornwallis's army. When I entered Little York I was most agreeably surprised at meeting my former companions; and more so when a pass was put into my hands, giving me the privilege of ten miles of the country round while I behaved well and orderly. This pass which serjeant Connor gave me at this time was like a sweet refreshing gale from Zion's top.[15] I was then conducted to a hut, which my poor loving comrades had built for me in their village before my arrival. Here I remained some time, visiting my former companions from hut to hut; but I was astonished at the spirit of industry which prevailed among them. Men, women, and even the children were employed making lace, buckles, spoons, and exercising other mechanical trades which they had learned during their captivity. They had very great liberty from the Americans, and were allowed to go round the country and sell their goods; while the soldiers of lord Cornwallis's army were closely confined in their pen. I perceived that they had lost that animation which ought to possess the breast of the soldier. I strove, by every argument, to rouse them from their lethargy. I offered to head any number of them, and make a noble effort to escape into New York, and join our comrades in arms; but all my efforts proved ineffectual.[16] Some Christians may be compared to these soldiers of general Burgoyne's army, when once they get into good quarters or meet with a rich booty, they are spoiled for fighting ever after. These prisoners of general Burgoyne's army spend their life in this

15. This sentence is from the commonplace book. Richard Connor was a sergeant in the 9th Regiment. WO 12/2653, TNA.

16. A June 1781 return of Convention Army troops shows just over 500 men remaining, along with almost 200 wives. List of British Prisoners Brought to Lancaster by Major Baily the 16th June 1781. Peter Force Papers, Series IX Reel 106 p. 675-685, Library of Congress.

village that some lazy people do in a market, that stand gazing about them without buying or selling. They slipped their opportunity, and if opportunities be not catched in the very nick, they are irrecoverably lost.[17] As for my own part, I was determined to make the attempt. I well knew, from experience, that a few companions would be highly necessary. Accordingly I sent word of my intention to seven men of the 23d regiment who were confined in the penn, and that I was willing to bring them with me. I believe in all the British army that these men (three serjeants and four privates) could not have been excelled for courage and intrepidity. They rejoiced at the idea; and by the aid of some of Burgoyne's army, they were enabled, under cover of a dark night, to scale their fence and assemble in my hut. I sent word of my intention to my commanding officer, captain Saumarez of the 23d*, and likewise the names of the men whom I purposed to bring with me. As my money was almost expended, I begged of him to advance me as much as convenient. He immediately sent me a supply.

It was on the 1st of March, 1782, that I set off with my party. My pass which had been procured from the American commander would only protect us to Susquehannah River which was not further than ten miles: we therefore marched those ten miles free from any dread of being apprehended. But when we arrived at the river, which was about a mile in breadth, we found that it could not be crossed on the ice, as it had thawed all that day. However when the evening drew on it began to freeze again, which encouraged us to remain until morning, under the hope that it would then be hard enough to bear us. At this place I found a man who had deserted from the Royal Welch Fuzileers about two years before. He seemed at first very shy of us; but after a little conversation he began to be more free. He acquainted us that since his desertion he had been roving

*Lately assistant quarter master general, and inspector of militia in the Island of Guernsey. [Editor: Captain Thomas Saumarez of the 23rd Regiment.]

17. These sentences, from "Some Christians," are from the commonplace book.

"Encampment of the convention army at Charlotte Ville in Virginia after they had surrendered to the Americans." Roger Lamb was never held in this circa 1779 hut camp for prisoners captured at Saratoga, but it may be similar to those he spent time in after his capture at Yorktown. Library of Congress.

about the country working very hard for his livelihood, and further, that, finding himself universally despised by the Americans, he had become very uneasy in his mind. Perceiving him well acquainted with the country, and possessing a thorough knowledge of all the loyal inhabitants, I thought in our present situation, he would be a valuable acquisition to us as a guide. In consequence, I held out to him every inducement, which I imagined might persuade him to accompany us. I urged, that we would as soon as we arrived at New York, intercede with Sir Henry Clinton for his pardon, which we had no doubt whatever would be immediately granted. He was also made thoroughly acquainted with the considerable rewards which he would receive both from the commander in chief, and from ourselves. After much entreaty, and supplying him with repeated drams of peach whiskey, he at last consented to guide us through Pennsylvania and the Jerseys, with which part of the country, and the temper of its inhabitants he seemed perfectly acquainted.

As it had froze all night, we ventured to cross the river at daylight the next morning. Though the ice was exceeding weak, and broken up in many places, the love of liberty had such a powerful effect, that we ventured with the firmest resolution, although the ice cracked under our feet every step we took, while we marched in Indian file. Having crossed this mighty river, we held a consultation what was best to be done. We had exceeded the bounds of my pass, and consequently were liable to be arrested in our process by the first party of American soldiers we met, or by any of the inhabitants who were disaffected; and even the loyalists, who might have succoured an individual or two, would most probably be fearful of giving assistance to such a party. Our guide, the deserter, informed as, that it would be impossible for us to march a mile further, unless we divided—that nine in number were too many together, as such a body of British soldiers would soon spread an alarm through the country and cause immediate pursuit. He also strongly advised us to change our regimental clothes for colored ones.[18] We all saw the propriety of this advice; with aching hearts we took leave of each other. I divided the party; serjeant Collins of the 23d, (a brave soldier, and a sensible man,)[19] took three men under his care, and I took the remaining four and our guide. We parted with great reluctance; but in full expectation of meeting each other at New York. The party which I commanded lay all day in the woods: but in the evening our guide brought us to the house of one of the king's friends, (the loyalists were so termed in America) where we changed our regimental clothes for very bad colored ones. There we remained until eleven o'clock, when, favored by the night, we began our march towards Lancaster. We kept in the woods as much as possible, and about the dawn of morning arrived at a small village. We entered into a house under the hope of procuring some refreshment. Almost

18. "Colored ones," civilian clothing of various colors.

19. Charles Collins, a sergeant in the 23rd Regiment of Foot. Muster rolls, 23rd Regiment of Foot, WO 12/3960, TNA.

immediately we perceived a man rising hastily out of bed. He dressed himself, and ran out of the house in great haste. Apprehensive, that he had ran out to alarm the neighbours, (indeed our appearance was very suspicious,) we left the house immediately, and took shelter in the woods; where we remained, almost perishing with hunger and cold until night. We then began our march. About the dawn of the succeeding day, we espied a large barn and a dwelling house contiguous. With one consent, we resolved to repose our weary limbs in this barn. We soon got in, and concealed ourselves under some sheaves of wheat which were in the loft. We had not remained in this place more than half an hour, when a boy came up to remove the corn for thrashing. He was greatly alarmed when he discovered us, and immediately ran down as fast he could. We thought it most prudent to follow him into the house, lest he should alarm the country. We entered the dwelling house almost as soon as him, saluted the farmer, and were desired to sit down. Our host ordered breakfast to be got ready, which consisted of ground Indian corn, boiled like stirabout.[20] No doubt, from the situation in which we had been discovered, and perhaps more from our looks, he perceived that we were hungry, and he was very right in his observation, for none of us had eaten any thing during more than fifty hours! After we had taken a hearty, I might add voracious breakfast, he said, "Gentlemen, I perceive who you are, and what is your intention, but I'll have nothing to do with you. Depart in peace." We offered him money; but he would not accept of it. We then thanked him warmly, and withdrew to our usual hiding place, the woods; where we remained for several hours. Our guide informed us, that ten miles further, on the great road leading to Philadelphia, lived one of the king's friends, from whom we should certainly receive entertainment, and who would probably furnish us with a list of

20. "Stirabout," a hasty pudding made of oatmeal boiled in water or mixed with meat drippings.

persons disposed, from principle, to assist us for forty miles on the way. Encouraged with this information, we set off towards the house in high spirits, which we reached at dusk in the evening. We sent our guide into the house, while we remained concealed in the orchard. He soon returned, and desired us to come in. We were received most cordially by the old man (Mr. Pim a quaker),[21] who bade us to sit down at a fine large fire, until refreshment could be got ready for us. He then, in the most feeling manner observed, "you know the great hazard I run in receiving you as friends. It is now (continued he) eight o'clock. I will let you remain under my roof till twelve. You must then depart." Having said this, a good supper was set before us, with plenty of cider. Mr. Pim was simple in his manners and frank and discreet in his speech. I wish it were as easy to be like, as it was impossible not to esteem him. Mr. Pim had a tear for pity and a hand as open as day for melting charity. This is not random assertion. It is not servile panegyric. The facts were felt by me and my poor companions in the hour of our distress, and are only mentioned to produce imitation.[22] The night proved very stormy, and the rain poured down like a deluge, which continued increasing every hour. However the hour of twelve arrived, and gratitude to our kind host, as well as fear for ourselves forbade our stay; and we resolutely faced the terrors of the midnight storm. What will not a captive endure to gain his freedom? The night was very dark: we therefore ventured to march on the main road to Philadelphia. It should have been mentioned, that before we departed from the house, our host kindly gave us a list of the king's friends who lived in our line of march, the nearest of whom was seventeen miles from his house: we therefore proceeded, notwithstanding the inclemency of the weather, with a degree of spirit animated by hope. The rain still continued to increase, which in a very short time drenched us to the skin; and, what rendered our journey more dis-

21. The parenthetical phrase is from the commonplace book.
22. This passage, from "Mr. Pim was," is from the commonplace book.

tressing, in consequence of the great fall of water, was, that the road was exceeding deep. Our guide also began to murmur at the hardships which he endured: his shoes were almost worn out. Indeed all our shoes were in a wretched condition. They were so bad that we could scarcely keep them on our feet. We used every suggestion that could possibly encourage him to proceed; but his spirit at last failed, and he declared, that he was unable to go any further with us: adding, with a deep sigh, "Perhaps, after all my hardships, if I should succeed, and get into New York, I shall not get my pardon." Just as he had pronounced these words, we espied a small hovel on the road side, and a house at a very little distance from it. We therefore, in order to keep him in temper, agreed to shelter ourselves from the storm under this hovel; assuring him at the same time that we would provide him a pair of shoes, and give him the best clothes we had in exchange for his bad ones. We drew near to the house, in order to rest our weary limbs; but, to our great mortification, we were saluted with the roaring and loud grunting of pigs which were in it. We soon found it necessary to march off as fast as we could from our noisy neighbours, lest by their outcries the inhabitants of the house should be alarmed. Thus circumstanced we were compelled to march on. At last we came within sight of a large barn. Here we again thought to take shelter, and were again disappointed; for, as we approached nearer, we perceived a light in it. Our guide began now to lose all his fortitude, declaring once more, that he was utterly unable to proceed any further. A large dunghill happened to be behind this barn, and as the last resource to humour our guide, we agreed to rest our limbs on it, and cover ourselves with the loose litter. Here we remained about half an hour, being unable to continue longer, from the effects of the extreme cold. We all felt severe pains in our bones, which were occasioned by the damp of the dung. It therefore became the general resolve to march on and gain our wished for house, which, from the distance we had already travelled, we judged could not be far off. We were further confirmed in this resolution by the morning breaking fast on us. At this place we arrived about the dawn. It was a tavern; but, to our unspeakable disappointment, we found that several American officers lodged in the house. Thus circumstanced, we were obliged immediately to proceed to another friend a few miles forward. We now thought it best to quit the great road, and turn off towards Valley-Forge. In the course of our march we fortunately happened to come to a shoemaker's dwelling, where we got all our shoes repaired, and having supplied our guide with a new pair, and given him our best clothes in exchange for his bad ones, and (above all) having supplied him with plenty of peach-whiskey, wherever we could procure it, he seemed determined for the present, to proceed with us to New York. In the evening we gained the house to which we had been directed. The lady who inhabited it, was a near relation of general Lee.[23] Both herself and husband were firmly attached to the royal cause. The house was situate on the banks of the Schuylkill. Here we halted for two days, during which time we were nobly entertained. At twelve o'clock on the night of the second day the master of the mansion provided a canoe, and sent his servant to put us across the river, giving us the name and place of abode of another friend. We now continued for some days going from one friend to another, still keeping our course towards New York. Early one morning we came to a river, which was very broad but only about four feet deep. In the middle of this river was a small island. We prepared ourselves to wade over. The morning was exceeding frosty which made the water very cold. Our guide now lost all his resolution. He declared with tears in his eyes "That his heart was almost broken with hardships, that he was sure he would never survive if he waded that river;" and all his fears about his pardon returned in full force upon him. We proposed to carry him over on our backs, to give him half the money we had, and renewed our former promises of interceding for him, and procuring his pardon; but all in vain. He turned about,

23. General Charles Lee of the Continental Army, who had been an officer in the British army before the war.

"Serjeant Lamb and his party persuading the deserter to accompany them as a guide into New York." This illustration from the commonplace book shows the escapees in early-1800s style civilian clothing. Methodist Historical Society of Ireland.

under great terror, and fled from us. We afterwards were informed, that this unfortunate man was, in the course of a few days, taken up, and the fact being proved, that he was seen conducting four men, supposed to be British soldiers, into New York, he was condemned, and hanged.

When we found it impossible to reclaim our guide, we waded across the river ourselves, and were almost deprived of the power of our limbs when we got on the other side. In the course of my life I have experienced galling excesses. O how often has my flesh fryed but here I was frozen. You may thank yourself Roger.[24] Our last protector had directed us to another friend, whose house was situate about two miles from this river. We therefore made what haste we could before the day advanced. We gained the hospitable mansion, and were concealed in the barn, and plentifully supplied with provisions. Thus far we had been successful in our enterprize. We were

24. These two sentences are from the commonplace book.

near the Delaware river, about twenty miles above Philadelphia. That river we were to cross in our progress. But in crossing it our protector could give us neither assistance or recommendation. He had no connexion on its shores which he durst trust. Soon however, as day closed we set off, and arrived on the banks of the Delaware about nine o'clock the same evening. We boldly ventured into a house to inquire for the ferry-house. Contrary to expectation we were kindly entertained, and informed that we were two miles from it. We remained at this place all night, and proceeded to the ferry-house early in the morning. A number of boatmen had just entered the house before us; they were employed in carrying wood to Philadelphia, and landed there (the house being a tavern) to refresh themselves. They were eight in number, and seemed, by their looks and conversation, to suspect who we were. As soon as we perceived this we called for some refreshment, and appeared cheerful and undismayed. After some time they withdrew into an inner room, to consult (as we supposed) how they were to attack and take us. We held a consultation, and were determined to part with our liberty at as dear a rate as we could. Just at this crisis, when we were preparing to act on the defensive, one of our party said, "Let us seize the ferry-boat, and make across the river." This proposal was immediately agreed to; and, after discharging our reckoning, we sallied out of the house, jumped into the ferry-boat and insisted on the negro who had the charge of her rowing us across with all expedition, on pain of instant death. This the terrified creature performed with such celerity, that we were half way over the Delaware before the alarm was given. The negro being in the boat with us, prevented their firing on us. We soon pulled to the opposite shore, and ran into the woods, where we were soon secure from all our pursuers, as we had above a mile and a half the start of them. We lay concealed in the thickest part of the wood that day; and at night proceeded in quest of a house to which we had been directed. After much search we found it, and were entertained a few hours, when we proceeded to the abode of another friend.

Such was the benevolent assistance which we received in this part of the country, that an imperative duty forces itself on me, here to notice the malignant assertions of Belsham, who says*, that when the British troops were retiring to Brunswick, through the Jerseys "the licentious ravages of the soldiery, particularly of the German mercenaries, during the time they were in possession of the Jerseys, had excited the utmost resentment and detestation of the inhabitants;" and that "such havoc, spoil, and ruin, were made by the forces under general Howe's personal inspection and command, as were well calculated to obviate the suspicion that any secret partiality to America yet remained in the breast of the English general."[25]

To this charge (with the most awful appeal for the verity of my assertion) I can aver, that in all the different places in America, through which I have marched as a soldier, been carried as a captive, or travelled in regaining my freedom, I never found people more strongly attached to the British government, than in the very place where Belsham says, "such havoc, spoil, and ruin, were made by the British forces." This we now experienced in a very great degree. These very inhabitants ventured their own lives to secure ours, and at the risque of their whole property, and the jeopardy of all their relatives and friends gave us the means of safe conduct into New York. Why Belsham cherished, and on almost every occasion manifested such inveterate malice against our commanders and soldiers in America, is matter of astonishment to me, and I might add, remains matter of mystery to the discerning and loyal part of the public. If the British troops in America had been capable of cooly and deliberately murdering his father, mother, and all his relatives, nay if they had actually perpetrated the horrid deed, he could scarcely have been more rancorous. An historian ought to record the *truth*, and the truth only, whether of friend or foe. The officers who served

*Memoirs of the Reign of George III. Vol. I. Page 388 and 408.

25. Lamb refers to British operations in New Jersey in the first half of 1777.

in the American campaigns were gentlemen (some of them noblemen, or noblemen's sons who have since succeeded to their hereditary titles) of the first families in the empire, for wealth as well as honor. Men who had no earthly temptation to such acts*, and whose high spirits independent of that circumstance would have revolted at the bare mention of the attrocities charged on them. However they ultimately failed in accomplishing the re-union of England and America, still it was the grand object of all their toils, both bodily and mental; and they were as far removed from "amassing fortunes by plunder and rapine," (as is asserted) by Ramsay, as Mr. Belsham and Ramsay are from acquiring fame by candor and truth. But to return to my narrative. We now entered into a country, which was full of American troops, and the nearer we proceeded to New York, the more numerous they were. This constrained us to act with great caution and circumspection: we made but short stages among our friends. On the 16th of March, we found ourselves within thirty miles of Staten Island, at which place was the British out-posts. Our American friend, in whose barn we lay concealed, advised us strongly to take a guide, which he said he could procure for us. To this we readily consented, and waited three days for our conductor. The black man and his wife whose hut was near the barn where we were concealed were very kind to us.[26] The wished for moment arrived; our guide came, the agreement was made, our friend procured me a bottle of strong spirits, and we set off with our conductor about nine o'clock at night, under the expectation of arriving before morning in the vicinity of Amboy; which town lay opposite Staten Island, being divided only by a river. In two hours march we came to a village which our guide told us we might safely march through, as the inhabitants were all in bed, and no American troops were stationed

*I am bold to assert that one British regiment was possessed of more property in gold, silver watches, &c. than was in general Washington's whole army: even the inhabitants were destitute of gold and silver.

26. This sentence is from the commonplace book.

in it. "But lest, said he, I should happen to be seen with you, I will take a circuit and meet you on the great road on the top of the hill, on the other side of the village." We consented to this plan and marched through the village unperceived, and arrived at the place appointed for meeting; there we remained, expecting our guide every moment; but after remaining two hours we gave up all hopes, and saw clearly that he had given us the slip. It snowed all the time very hard accompanied with a piercing north wind. Our clothes and shoes being all torn, made our situation, while we waited, almost insupportable: we at last came to the resolution of proceeding by ourselves, though we were entirely unacquainted upon what point of the compass Amboy lay. But the stars being rather bright we knew we could not be materially wrong if we proceeded due north. We marched very hard over a broken uneven ground, sometimes on the road and sometimes through the woods. At four o'clock in the morning one of our companions dropped down and declared with tears in his eyes, he was not able to proceed any farther: the soles of his shoes had been worn off and his feet were all bruised and cut. Indeed we were all much in the same way. We proposed to carry him by turns till daylight, when we would repose ourselves. "No," said he, "leave me here to die; for I am quite exhausted: if I live till morning, I will strive to creep to the next house; and if I survive, I will endeavour to follow you." This poor fellow was so overpowered by hunger and fatigue that he appeared to us when we parted from him to be an hospital of incurables.[27] We were greatly affected at parting with him. To me indeed it was peculiarly distressing, as he was one of the men I had brought in with me to New York from general Burgoyne's army, and was the man whom I have already mentioned, who understood several languages, and who was of so much service in effecting our escape.[28]

27. This sentence is from the commonplace book.
28. Probably William Gunn, who had been with Lamb in the 9th Regiment, joined the 23rd at the same time as Lamb, and did not remain a prisoner until the end of the war. Gunn deserted on August 5, 1783. Muster rolls, 23rd Regiment of Foot, WO 12/3960, TNA.

We marched on until the morning when we concealed ourselves in the woods, until the night came on. During this time we were without provisions. Soon as the evening set in we prepared as well as we could, for our march. About two o'clock in the morning we perceived a house, on the side of a narrow road, it was unconnected with any other building. Not knowing, where we were, we agreed to stop, and obtain all the information which we could. We rapped at the door, which was quickly opened by an old man, who with his wife were the only persons in the house. Without discovering who we were, we entered into conversation with them both. It came out, during our discourse, that he was a native of Dublin and had left it about thirty years before. Here my being a native of Ireland was of inestimable service to the whole party. As I could mention several places in Dublin, and many of the transactions which had happened in his time, he became highly pleased with my conversation, and with true native hospitality brought out provisions to entertain his countryman. From several of his answers which he gave to some of the questions which I occasionally, and I may say accidentally, put to him, I perceived he was a loyalist; but being unwilling to commit the whole party, I did not discover to him whom we were. Having gained all the information which we wanted, we left his house.

He had informed us where the American guards were stationed along the banks of the river, who could at all interfere with us, which was only the distance of two miles off. We immediately proceeded towards it, carefully avoiding the American posts. About an hour before day-light we arrived on its banks, and as soon as morning dawned, we saw with pleasure Staten Island. But a deep and broad river rolled between us and our place of refuge. We wandered up and down the shore in hope of finding a canoe or boat; but in vain. After a fruitless search for near an hour, the broad appearance of day much alarmed us, as we dreaded lest some of the American sentinels, who were posted along the coast, should discover us. In this dangerous situation, we held a consultation what was best to be done; when it was unanimously agreed to return to my countryman's house, discover

"The American friend bringing us provisions." Lamb's commonplace book includes this illustration of him and his three comrades hiding in a barn in Amboy, New Jersey. Methodist Historical Society of Ireland.

who we were and throw ourselves upon his protection. We returned, and were not disappointed: we found him to be a staunch loyalist. He observed, "The coast is full of troops—I will bring you to a place of concealment." He then conducted us to a thick part of a wood, while he went to two friends, who owned a boat, in which we could at night safely cross the river. There we remained until a late hour in the evening, when his two friends, with the boatmen, came to us; and having agreed for our passage, we proceeded to the boat. The river, where we had to cross, was more than three miles broad.

Our friends informed us, that an English sloop of war was stationed there, in order to intercept the American privateers and other craft, and likewise to keep the coast in alarm. We entered the boat with joy, and put off from the shore. They had not rowed a quarter of a mile, when the wind, which had hitherto been fair for us, changed against us, and blew very fresh. The boat, being very small, made a great deal of water.[29] This greatly alarmed the boatmen; and they immediately made for the shore from whence we came. When

29. "Made a great deal of water," took on water from waves washing over it.

we perceived what they were about, we insisted that they should turn the boat, and endeavour to gain the sloop; or, failing in that, row us across to Staten Island. They were greatly alarmed at our resolution; and declared, that it was impossible for a boat to live in that gale of wind; and that we should be all certainly lost, if we persisted in the attempt. But we were resolved to venture, and peremptorily commanded them to proceed. After beating against the wind and waves for near two hours, and being almost perished with wet and cold, we espied a square rigged vessel. The boatmen were apprehensive at first that she was an American privateer. However, as our boat was every moment in danger of sinking, we determined to make towards her. As we approached, we were hailed, and ordered to come along side. To our unspeakable joy, we saw British soldiers standing on the deck. Such was the effect of our sufferings, that we had almost lost the power of our limbs and speech: for when I was ordered down to the cabin to captain Skinner,[30] to give him an account who we were, I could not articulate a word. Perceiving my situation, he humanely ordered a large glass of rum to be given me. This soon brought me to my speech, and I then briefly recapitulated to him our whole story. The ship's company being informed that we were British soldiers who had escaped from the Americans, were eager to express their joy. We were ordered the best refreshments the vessel could afford. In the morning we were put on shore on Staten Island, with a letter to the captain's father, colonel Skinner,[31] who commanded a regiment of loyal Americans, and who was the commanding officer on Staten Island.

I need not tell the Reader what we felt when we were marching across the island, where we considered ourselves perfectly safe within the British lines. We waited on colonel Skinner, who immediately ordered a boat to convey us to New York. We landed at the wharf, and with cheerful steps marched to head quarters. When the

30. Probably John McGregor Skinner, lieutenant in the Royal Navy.

31. Cortland Skinner, brigadier general commanding the New Jersey Volunteers, a loyalist brigade.

inhabitants, and the soldiers in garrison, understood that we were three serjeants of the Royal Welch Fuzileers, they were struck with astonishment. We had had no opportunity of shaving ourselves for more than three weeks; our shoes were worn out; our clothes all in tatters; our looks wan and meagre. In short so wretched was our appearance, that they commiserated our condition, and with kind attention conducted us to the commander in chief. This was on the 23d of March, 1782.

Sir Henry Clinton received us with great kindness. We communicated to his excellency all the information of which we were possessed, which in any manner tended to the good of the service. After this, we were sent to receive the usual bounty, which was given as an encouragement to those soldiers who made good their escape. After the officer who was appointed to pay us had entered my name in the book, he turned his eye to the top of the first page, and said, "Here is the same name of a non-commissioned officer of the 9th regiment, one of the first who had made his escape from general Burgoyne's army, more than four years ago." I answered, "I am the man." On which he replied, "if you arc the man, your colonel (colonel Hill) who was exchanged, and went to England, has left here all your arrears of pay." "But," added he, "you must prove that you are the identical person." This I soon did, as there were officers both of the 9th and 23d regiments, who knew me well at that time in New York. In consequence, I received a very considerable sum, which was due to me. I then wrote out this narrative, and presented it to major Mackenzie, deputy quarter master general*. The major recommended me to brigadier general Birch,[32] the commandant of New York, and I was appointed his first clerk, for which I had a

*Now colonel Mackenzie, and secretary to the military college, London. [Editor: Frederick Mackenzie was an officer in the 23rd Regiment of Foot who was serving as Deputy Adjutant General in New York in 1781. His diaries, among the most significant primary sources available, have been published as *Diary of Frederick Mackenzie*, Cambridge: Harvard University Press, 1930; reprinted New York: Arno Press, 1970.]

32. Samuel Birch, brigadier general and commandant of city of New York.

good salary. The major's kindness did not stop there; but through his interest I was made, adjutant to the Merchants Corps of volunteers,[33] who were then on permanent duty in the town.

At this place, during two months, I enjoyed a comfortable respite from the hard duty to which I had been accustomed: the only repose, I may truly say, which I had during the eight years I was in America.

Colonel Balfour, having, arrived in New York from Charlestown, it being evacuated,[34] ordered me to proceed to King's Bridge, the out post of the British army, and take charge of the recruits of the 23d regiment, who were doing duty there; to which place I repaired accordingly.

The Reader will doubtless feel some anxiety for the fate of the party which I left on the banks of the Susquehannah River. These poor fellows, after enduring innumerable hardships, and travelling through the woods for some hundreds of miles, were unfortunately taken prisoners in Pennsylvania, and confined in Philadelphia jail, the foundation of which they undermined, and the whole four came safe into New York, the latter end of April. Much about the same time, my former companion, whom I had left on the road, likewise arrived at New York, conducted by the last guide, who had divided from us in passing through the village. Thus, though by different routes, the whole party which I took with me from Little York, arrived safe at the British head quarters.

When I reflect on the hardships which I endured, the dangers which I escaped from my first setting out from Gloucester, after our army was taken prisoners, in a march of perhaps not less than one thousand miles, through a wilderness interspersed with swamps, I feel (and senseless must I be if I did not feel it) a degree of thankfulness to that Providence, who, not only preserved my life in several

33. The New York City Militia, a battalion composed of merchants and traders.
34. Charleston, South Carolina, was evacuated by the British Army on December 14, 1782.

hard fought battles, skirmishes, &c. but also guided my footsteps through those desart tracks, and brought me in safety once more among my friends. It is true, I can state the fact in the language of the great heathen poet:

"From the din of war,
Safe I returned without one hostile scar;
Though balls in leaden tempests rained around,
Yet innocent they flew, and guiltless of a wound."[35]

But I must acknowledge as a Christian, (however I may by some persons be charged with enthusiasm for it) that in all these wonderful events of my past life, I see and adore an higher direction—an arm Omnipotent which has been my safe guard; and penetrated with the recollection of which I may truly say—"O God the Lord, the strength of my salvation; Thou hast covered my head in the day of battle."

35. From *The Odyssey of Homer*, Alexander Pope, trans.

CHAPTER TEN

[Return to Great Britain]

The Author's Return, &c.

I SAILED FROM SANDY HOOK on the 5th of December 1783,[1] and on the 17th of January, 1784, landed at Portsmouth with the 23d regiment: from that place we marched to Winchester. For some time after the Regiment came to England from America I had no intention of leaving the Army, as I was in a situation of making money, but an order came from the War Office, for the Regiment to be reduced according to the peace establishment. At this time I was employed to fill up the soldiers discharges, which were signed by the Colonel before they were sent to me. The soldiers were asked "How long have you served" their answer would be seven or eight years more than they really were in the service, this they said in order that they might the more readily pass the Board by having a longer servitude. I then wrote the number of years they mentioned. But in filling up my own discharge I wrote Twelve just the number I really did serve. It is a false notion to think soldiers are served by putting down in their papers more years than they actually were in the service. No it is bringing a curse on them by lying and perjury! They

1. The British Army evacuated New York City on November 25, 1783, but it was several days before favorable winds allowed the transports carrying troops to leave New York harbor.

are obliged to swear in a most solemn manner before a Magistrate every quarter of a year, that they have served the number of years specified in their discharge. And I do not wonder at the misery some of these poor old men undergo after leaving the Army seeing that the curse of lying and perjury are upon them.

I will just remark here that there was a great want of discipline in suffering an non-commissioned officer to fill up the mens discharges according to his pleasure, there ought to have been a commissioned officer appointed for this duty who with the greatest scrutiny should inspect the Regimental books, and enter exactly in their discharges the number of years each man served.

While thus engaged a thought occurred "Now is the time to get your discharge." This impression was so strong upon my mind that I went to the Colonel and interceded with him for my discharge. At that time I had very great privileges allowed me in the army, and was making money fast; but peace being proclaimed through all Europe, I thought it my duty to come home to my friends in Dublin, after an absence of near twelve years, during which time I had served my country to the best of my power. Colonel Balfour, who commanded the regiment (well knowing that I was making money in my situation,) kindly and humanely reasoned with me, in order to prevail on me to remain in the army. He was at first greatly displeased at my request and reasoned with me, he said "you have no trade and Ireland is a very poor place; you had better remain where you are. Your are comfortably situated, and you are making money. Go to your quarters think on what I have said, come to me in two hours and let me know your determination." During the two hours my mind was greatly agitated, my heart was ready to break with sorrow at the idea of leaving the Regiment, where I was so kindly used, and had received such indulgences; yet under all these feelings that word followed me, "Now is the time to get your discharge." I went again to the Colonel and said—"Sir I would be thankful if you will let me go, I have an old mother in Dublin who I long to see before she dies"—He seemed unwilling at first to hear me, but on my pressing the matter, he seeing my determination was fixed, he signed my discharge and in displeasure said—"Here take you discharge and fill it up."

I marched up to London with a number of my companions, in order to pass the board. When the board sat I was considered as too young to receive the pension; and likewise that I had not been long enough in the service.[2] It is true, the general officers who composed the board at that time were unacquainted with me; and besides, as nothing was mentioned in my discharge but the time of my servitude, and "that I was discharged," they could not possibly be aware of the nature and extent of my services, or the claims which I possessed on the bounty of my sovereign. I cannot help but pause here, and wonder at the preventing goodness of God in overruling me when filling up my own discharge. Perhaps upon that very act depended my future happiness or misery, for had I put down twenty years in the room of twelve, what would that have done for me? Why probably I might have passed the Board and then I would have to swear to that lie. It is true I was greatly grieved at my own folly as I thought when I found I was rejected for not having a sufficient number of years in my discharge, when I could so easily have done it before I brought it to the Board. How often do we think that some things which happen to us in life will prove very injurious to us, but they often turn out in the end to be for our real good.[3]

Lieutenant Calvert*, of the 23d being then in London, I communicated my disapointment to him. He was sorry for me; and said, "Any thing that lies in my power I will do for you." He advised me to remain in London until another board would sit; but I was de-

*Now major general Calvert and adjutant general of the British forces.

---

2. The out-pension examining board typically awarded pensions to soldiers who had served for at least twenty years, or who had acquired disabilities as a result of their service. Lamb went before the board on March 8, 1784. Pension Admission Books, WO 116/8, TNA. Form more on army pensions, see Hagist, *Noble Volunteers*, 244-253.

3. The three paragraphs above are primarily from the commonplace book, with a few sentences from *Journal of the American War*.

BY Major Thomas Gibbings

Commanding His Majesty's Twenty Third Regiment of

INFANTRY,

whereof Major General Richard Grenville is Colonel.

THESE are to Certify, That the Bearer hereof Thomas Parks Private has served well and faithfully in the above-named Regiment, for Fifteen Years & Seven Months and in other Regiments, according to the annexed Return.

THE said Thomas Parks is now hereby discharged, having first received his Pay, Arrears of Pay, Clothing, &c. and all other just Demands whatsoever, from the Time of his Enlisting into said Regiment, till the Day of his Discharge, as appears by his Receipt on the other Side.

HE is discharged, having an obstinate Chronic Rheumatism, & was wounded in the head, at Guildford Court House, North Carolina, America, on the 15 March 1781

as more fully appears by the Surgeon's Certificate, describing the Origin, Nature and State of his Complaint, and why unfit for Service; and is hereby recommended as a fit Object of His Majesty's Royal Bounty of *Kilmainham* Hospital.

SERVICE.

CORPS.	Serj^t. Major.	Qu. Ma. Serj^t.	Serjeant.	Drummer.	Corporal.	Private.	Total Service.
	Years.	Years.	Years.	Years.	Years.	Years.	Years.
23^d Reg^t	"	"	"	"	"	15 7	—
Total							

DESCRIPTION.

NAME.	Height.		Age.	Trade.	Where Born.	County.
	Feet.	Inch.				
Thomas Parks	5	9	41	Labourer	Birmingham	Warwick

Given under my Hand, and Seal of the Regiment, at Armagh this 19 Day of October 1792

N. B. When a Soldier is discharged on Account of Wounds or Hurts, the Officer giving the Discharge is to specify when, where, and how they were received, whether on Duty or otherwise.

T Gibbings Major 23 Reg^t

The 1793 discharge of Thomas Parks, soldier in the 23rd Regiment, wounded at Guilford Courthouse in 1781. In 1784 Lamb was tasked with filling out printed forms similar to this one, entering each soldier's name, place of birth, and other data. The format of the forms differed from year to year, but the information recorded on them was similar. WO 97/431/68, The National Archives.

termined not to wait. Lieutenant Calvert was well acquainted with me; we had served together in America for some years; I have frequently had the honor of obeying his command, and of fighting by his side in many battles and skirmishes. Even twenty-five years after these services, he was not unmindful of me; for when I took the liberty of writing to him in September 1808, he kindly answered the letter, and renewed his former acts of friendship by recommending me to the duke of York.

Attachments of persons in the army to each other terminate but with life, the friendship of the officer continues with the man who has fought under his command, to the remotest period of declining years, and the old soldier venerates his aged officer far more than perhaps he did in his youthful days: it is like friendship between school-boys, which encreases in manhood, and ripens in old age.

I left London on the 15th of March, and landed in Dublin on the 19th, to the inexpressible joy of an aged mother, two sisters, and other relations, who had long given up every hope that I was alive.

It might be thought the writer ought to offer some account of his subsequent life. He is sensible the humble path of laborious obscurity in which he has proceeded since he ceased to be a Soldier, carries forward little but unimportant features, and nothing to give it a due value for Public perusal. War, however dreadful, throws a degree of interest on this Memoir. Peace, although truly amiable in appearance, is too silent and sedentary to attract the curiosity of inquisitive human beings.

It was on the 19th March 1784 I landed in Dublin after being twelve years in the army.

Very few persons I suppose in the Methodist Society have published more concerning themselves than I have, yet there is a manifest difference in writing the life of a man as a soldier and as a Christian. In the first it is usual to notice every instance of courage, danger &c in order to set forth the man; but in the latter it should be the aim of the writer to display the power and efficacy of divine grace, in order that the Redeemer might be exalted, and have all the praise of his own work. In both cases we may exclaim with the Psalmist "Blessed be the Lord our strength who teacheth our hands to war and our fingers to fight."

In 1809 and 1811 I published two volumes which contain my adventures, dangers and troubles while a soldier, in those volumes I

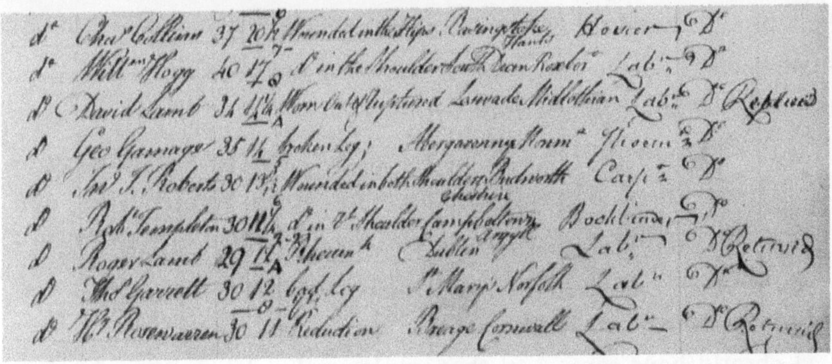

Because he did not have a trade, Roger Lamb (listed third from the bottom) was recorded as a "labourer" when he went before the pension examining board on March 8, 1784. He was 29 years old, with twelve years of service. The National Archives.

have not touched upon my Christian warfare, the reason was I wrote for the public, and I well knew that the natural man receiveth not the things of the spirit of God for they are foolishness unto him, neither can he know them because they are spiritually discerned.

I have for some years past read several authors on practical divinity, many passages in their writings I thought worthy to be noticed, these with my Christian experience I have put down in this form, perhaps they may be useful to some who are acquainted with the workings of God upon their own souls. Tho' to others who are entire strangers to such things those kinds of narrations will generally appear foolishness.

This account I do not intend to publish, but if after my death my surviving friends think it will be for the glory of God, and the good of souls to make them known, they may add it to my Memoir which is already published.

Not that I think any child of God is either afraid or ashamed to lay open his heart before his brethren while living and my Christian friends in Dublin can bear me witness that I have not concealed the goodness of God to me when proper opportunities have occurred.

It has often been remarked that to begin in the good way is well, to continue in the path is better, but if he persevere unto the end best of all. Therefore it may be best to wait till the soldier puts off his harness and see the issue of the combat before it can be pronounced what grace has done for him.

After I landed in Dublin it pleased the Lord by the ministry of the Methodist preachers to convince me of sin, righteousness and judgment, the thoughts of death and eternity filled me with fear, I was burthened with the weight of my misery and my heart was humbled before the Lord.

I should have remarked that while in the Army I was I was a most extraordinary sinner. I had almost filled up the measure of my iniquities. Behold my picture. There was nothing I had but the devil had dominion over it; he ruled the whole man; my eyes were blinded. All my apprehension were shapen by Satan. I looked on sin with the devil's spectacles. I saw nothing in its native colours, but was under a continual delusion my very wisdom was devilish or devil-like. If the bait of honour or pleasure were presented to me, I skipt after it as a dog would after a crust. I feared not the dreadful wages which the Great God threatened. As sometimes you will see a Spaniel so greedy of a bone that he will leap into the very river for it, if you throw it thither, and by that time he comes thither it is sunk, and he gets nothing but a mouthful of water for his pains.

Satan keeps his slaves full handed with work. The sinner grinds and he is filling the hopper; that the mill may not stand idle.

I remember with trembling astonishment the condition my poor soul was then in. The devil was with me as soon as I awoke filling my wretched heart with some wicked thoughts, which as a morning draught kept me from any savour of good, that might be breathed on me by others in the day time. All the day long he watched me as the master would do his man that he feared would run away.

My great expectation was happiness and my great folly what that I thought to obtain it by gratifying my evil desire. O how foolish! I might as well seek to cure a wound in my body by applying a plaister to my garment, as to seek to ease a wounded spirit by the treasures, pleasures and enjoyments of this world.

Earthly things are empty and unsatisfying we may have too much but never enough of them, they oft breed loathing but never content. How can a man be content with the guilt of sin on his soul, this will spoil all his mirth. You know all our dancing of a child when some pin pricks it, will not make it quiet or merry.

Quarter Master Burgess (of the first Regiment of horse) who is now a Methodist preacher, was at that time in Dublin.[4] He was a nursing father to me, he frequently followed, advised and instructed me, his temper and upright walk had a good effect upon my mind.

How well it is when persons professing godliness endeavour to spread religious knowledge and enforce their instructions with pious examples.

When under the preaching of God's word I frequently wept, and resolved to live to God's glory. But alas! To will was present with me, but how to perform that which was good I found not. For the good that I will I did not but the evil which I would not that I did. The language of my soul was

My reason this, my passion that pursuit.
I see the right and I approve it to,
Condemn the wrong and yet the wrong do.
Resolutions made in my own strength
Were only as the spiders web

For more than two years I was kept under the iron bondage of satan at some times sinning and sometimes repenting. My life was a burden to me, for I felt perfectly miserable.

It was on the 26th of May 1786 that God first spoke peace to my soul on the memorable morning being greatly distressed in my mind I retired into the fields to pray. I had not been long in this blessed exercise, when I felt the love of God shed abroad in my heart thro' the Holy Spirit given unto me. At that happy moment I cried out "If love be heaven, if peace be heaven, if joy be heaven I have it.

4. For more on this man, see William P. Burgess, "Memoir of the Rev. Joseph Burgess," *Wesleyan-Methodist Magazine* 3rd Series Vol. 19 (July 1840), 537-556.

A Redeeming God is my favourite theme and the name of Jesus enraptures my grateful soul."

I now devoted my time, my thoughts, words, works, gifts, business, wife and children constantly to the Lord, and I felt every moment my sacrifice was accepted.[5] I had uninterrupted converse with God. My heart was entirely free to worship the Lord. He was the life of my soul and my portion for ever. His presence did not forsake me for a moment. He held a helpless worm in his hand, and blessed me with the beams of his glory. I shall remark here that the sabbath days were the sunshine days of my calendar—how my soul welcome them.

I continued in this happy frame of soul till the beginning of the year 1787 when that dirty planet the earth got between me and my Sun of righteousness. Let me entreat all who read this never force God to withdraw from you as a friend does whom he is grieved by unkind behaviour. You may depend upon it that God will change his favours when we change our conduct.

For several months my mind was dissipated by triffles or congealed by indolence. At that time there was a blessed revival in the city, the venerable Mr. Wesley paid his annual visit.[6] In attending the word preached I was roused from my lethargy to hear and think. I now discovered I was shorn of my strength. I am sure I felt that godly sorrow working repentance to salvation. O what awefulness it wrought in me, yea, what clearing of myself, yea, what indignation, yea what fear, yea what vehement desire, yea, what zeal, yea what revenge: in all things I endeavoured to approve myself to be clear in this matter. Well indeed I know that godly sorrow lessens natural. My conversion from sin to God was clear, sound, and decided. For some time before this I had a strong conviction of actual

5. Roger Lamb married Jane Crumer on January 15, 1786; she apparently died, and he married Ann Young in 1805. There is inconclusive evidence of another marriage in between these two. For more on Lamb's family and life in Dublin, see Kenneth Ferguson, "Roger Lamb: Soldier and Writer, Schoolmaster at Whitefriar Street," *Bulletin of the Methodist Historical Society of Ireland* Vol. 23 No. 2 (2018), 107-190.

6. John Wesley, theologian and Methodist leader.

sin, and of the natural depravity which is its source—of the moral helplessness which is its concomitant, and of the awful exposure of divine wrath and endless ruin, which is its effect. I felt Godly sorrow, the result of this conviction, working repentance towards God, with earnest prayer for pardon and grace and other fruits meet for such repentance.

Before I left the Army I often thought of the situation of a School Master, and I used to say—"When I get my discharge I will set up a school and instruct children"—After I was discharged and received the pardoning love of God, I made my request know to him for this employment. He graciously heard my request and made my way so plain that under all my subsequent trials and temptations, I have been supported by the consideration—I have received my employment in answer to prayer. It is true I am often discouraged at the opposition which the devil and the hearts of children make against my efforts. The besetting sins of children are self will, disobedience, lying and a settled inattention to the things of God. How natural is it for children to connect the idea of study with that of hardship—of happiness with gluttony—and of pleasure with loitering—feasting—or sleeping.

I feel a self abasing sense of my own insufficiency for any good word, or work and am grieved at my inability to do them good.

Two things I have had in view from the beginning. First—To endeavour to make my scholars useful to Society by teaching them to read, write and cipher, and secondly to promote their eternal interests. These two points I have endeavoured to pursue according to my ability, and I cannot help saying (although it may seem a breach of modesty) that my labours have not been in vain, and I am fully persuaded that God will answer for me in that day when he makes up his jewels.

Since that period I have been frequently asked by various friends to whom I related the circumstances of the battle of Guildford Court House, why I did not apply to marquis Cornwallis for some situation, when lord lieutenant of Ireland, in the year 1798? My answer was, and is, that at that time I had a young family, and was moreover tolerably well settled. I knew his excellency would have recognized me immediately, as I had been employed by him during the campaign to write the duplicates of his dispatches. A commission in a marching regiment would most probably have been my reward, which I could not have accepted, from the state of my health as well as the reasons assigned.

One day in the month of September 1808 looking over a newspaper, I read an order from the war office signed "Henry Calvert Adjutant general". It immediately occurred to me, that this officer served in the 23rd and had always shewed himself my friend. I mentioned this circumstance to some of my family who advised me to write to him, upon which I sent him the following letter.

> Dublin 26th September 1808
>
> Sir
>
> Sensible as I am of the very important and honourable station you fill in his Majesty's service, and being an old soldier who had often the honour of obeying your command, and of fighting by your side in America, I have taken the liberty to address these lines to you. I am encouraged to hope you will not be offended at my boldness, as you were pleased to express your approbation of my conduct when serving with you in the 23rd Foot, in the American War. The last time I saw your honour in London in 1784, you were pleased to say, that any thing that lay in your power in which you could serve me you would cheerfully do. Permit me honoured Sir to state the following particulars.
>
> I enlisted in the 9th Foot in the year 1773 being then near 17 years of age; and was very soon promoted a non commissioned officer. In 1776, I went to America, under the command of general Burgoyne, and was taken prisoner with the British army October 1777 at Saratoga. I remained a prisoner till November 1778, when in the face of danger surrounded by American guards, I made my escape and was one of the

first of general Burgoyne's army that entered the British lines in New York. I gave very important intellegence concerning the American Army, and was rewarded by the commander in Chief Sir Henry Clinton. I might have returned to Great Britain at that time, but I rather chose to serve his Majesty in America; therefore inlisted into the 23rd Foot then lying in New York. Very soon after I joined the regiment I was promoted to be a serjeant, and served in several important expiditions till the latter end of the year 1779, when the regiment was ordered to South Carolina; after the taking of Charles Town the 23rd Foot remained under the command of that brave and experienced commander general Cornwallis. I had the honour of carrying the regimental colours on the 16th of August 1780 where his lordship with the British troops defeated a superior army of the Americans under the command of general Gates near Camden. After this engagement Captain Champagne who commanded the 23rd Foot at that time, was pleased to appoint me temporary surgeon to the regiment (having had some little knowledge of physic) till a professional gentleman from Charles Town could be procured. In this situation I contined some time with general approbation. After a series of hard toil, incessant effort, and stubborn action our little army penetrated as far as Guildford Court House in North Carolina. Here we met Mr. Green with 6000 American troops whom we attacked and defeated on the 15th of March 1781. In this engagement (the hardest fought battle I believe we had in America) I had the heart felt pleasure of being instrumental of saving Lord Cornwallis from being taken prisoner. I am however confident, that there was not a man in our brave little army but would have acted in the same manner which I did, were he in my place. After this engagement we marched into Virginia and arrived at York Town. Here we were surrounded by the united armies of America and France. The 23rd regiment then under the command of Captain

Apthorp occupied a very important redoubt on the right a mile in front of the British fortified camp. In this honourable post we remained covering our army, and nobly resisting the enemies united attack for several weeks. Our general after some time was induced to open a treaty with general Washington.

Permit me to say, that during this campaigne whenever any dangerous enterprize was to be performed by any part of the regiment, I was always one of the first serjeants picked out to carry it into execution, and you well know, Sir, how often we have distinguished our selves in many bold manoevers.

When a prisoner the second time, I was often strongly solicited and promised many rewards if I would desert and remain in the country, but I was determined to die sooner than serve any State hostile to Great Britain. I could not bear the idea of even remaining a prisoner. I communicated my thoughts to Mr. Gardiner our Quarter Master who mentioned it to our commanding officer, and he advised me to take as many men with me as I could, and gave me money for that service. I picked out three serjeants and four privates brave resolute fellows, four of these men were unfortunately taken on their way and confined in Philadelphia jail the foundation of which they undermined and made their escape. We all arrived safe at the British head quarters at New York in May 1782.

On our coming to New York general Birch who was commandant of the City was pleased to appoint me his Clerk and adjutant to the merchants corps, which was then doing duty in the town. Shortly after Colonel Balfour came to New York from Charles Town and ordered me to take charge of a party of men belonging to our regiment then lying at King's Bridge. After peace was made between Great Britain and America and the remains of our regiment were collected together on Long Island, the officers then in the regiment who were well acquainted with my conduct very much desired that I should be promoted serjeant major of the regiment as there was a vacancy. In this I was superceded thro' the interference of Miss Peters, and a favourite waiting woman whose husband (then a serjeant) got the promotion.

The Officers however willing to do me good, appointed me sutler to the regiment and likewise conductor of their mess, in which situation I continued till we arrived in England.

I received my discharge at Winchester from Colonel Balfour (who always behaved like a father to me) and came up to London with several serjeants and privates in order to pass the Board. The general officers who presided thought I was too young to be admitted an out pensioner, by this means I was deprived of his Majesty's Royal bounty.

Since that time I have remained in the City of Dublin in the situation of a School Master. I was strongly urged by my friends to Memorial Marquis Cornwallis when Lord Lieutenant of Ireland, but being then in easy circumstances, I declined making any application to him.

I am now in the 52 year of my age, the infirmities of life are beginning to multiply fast, and the consequences of my exertions in the Royal service are more perceivable every year. My wife and six children depend on my labour under Providence.

I feel no small degree of satisfaction that it is to your honour I submit these lines, as you are well acquainted with most of the particulars I have stated. I cherish an humble confidence from a sense of your former friendship and kindness to me that you will not be unmindful of the soldier who with all his might contributed to the defence of that government which is the envy of the world.

I am
&c &c

Roger Lamb.

N. B. I can be well recommended by several respectable citizens of Dublin as a loyal subject and an honest man.

I received a letter from the general in which he acknowledged the receipt of mine and kindly expressed a wish to serve me, that he had consulted on my case with Colonel Mackenzie who as well as himself was my well wisher but that it did not occur to either of them in what manner they could serve me; that he would refer my letter to the Adjutant general of Ireland in case he should have the opportunity of giving me some employment in that country.

A few days after I received a note from general Clinton Quarter Master general of Ireland requesting me to call at his Office.[7] I waited on the general and the following conversation took place.

General Clinton.

Mr. Lamb I have receive a letter from general Calvert and Colonel Mackenzie, recommending you for some employment in this Country: pray what situation are you in at present?

Lamb

I am Master of the Methodist Free School in Whitefriar Street.

General Clinton

What salary, and what family have you?

Lamb

I have sixty pounds a year, and I have a wife and six children.

Genl. Clinton

We shall want a Master for the Hibernian School shortly, suppose we were to appoint you for that situation you must not assume the office of the chaplain? (smiling)

Lamb

I would not Sir. But I hope my being a Methodist would not disqualify me for holding either a military or a civil situation under government.

7. William Henry Clinton, son of Gen. Henry Clinton under whom Lamb had served in America.

Genl. Clinton

Indeed Mr Lamb I think every man should chuse the best religion he could, nevertheless I think the Methodists carry religious matter too far.

Lamb

Sir I was a very wicked man before I heard the Methodist preachers, but thro' their instrumentality I have been reformed. Here Sir is a recommendation from John David Latouche Esqr. An eminent banker in this city.

Mr. Latouche's recommendation which the general read: "I have known Mr. Roger Lamb, School Master for several years and believe him to be a man of excellent principles and conduct and who fulfills his duty belonging to his situation in life with credit to himself and with advantage to those committed to his care. J. D. Latouche"

Castle Street Octr. 20th 1808.

Lamb

And give me leave to say Sir, that I know the Methodist are very loyal to his Majesty's person and government.

General Clinton

I do think Mr. Lamb that if our clergy would do their duty, there would be no need of Methodist preachers.

Lamb

I think so too Sir.

General Clinton

Indeed it would be very grateful to my mind to serve you, but it does not occur to me in what manner it can be done. Come with me to the Commissary general, I will consult with him about you. This is Mr. Lamb Colonel Handfield.

Colonel Handfield

Lamb—Lamb—I think I know that name, did you not make your escape into New York from genl. Burgoyne's army?

Lamb

I made my escape into New York, from general Burgoyne's and Lord Cornwallis's army.

Colonel Handfield.

I remember you very well, I paid you money by order of the commander-in-Chief.

Lamb

I was rewarded by Sir Henry Clinton, and Sir Guy Carleton in New York. He then asked me several questions concerning my School, The Methodist society and the Stranger Friend Society &c &c

General Clinton to Colonel Handfield

Mr. Lamb can be very well recommended by respectable persons in Dublin, and genl. Calvert and Colonel Mackenzie speak very highly of him.

Colonel Handfield

What was your object in writing to general Calvert?

Lamb

My object in writing to the general was that through his interest I might be appointed an officer in the Royal Hospital at Kilmainham.

Colonel Handfield

It would require great interest indeed to be appointed a Captain there, and none but those who had been commissioned officers could expect it, beside you were not long in the army.

Lamb

Sir I have seen very hard service for eight years in America and was always approved by my officers for good conduct.

Colonel Handfield

We are going to apply to Parliament for a grant to enable us to build a range of additional buildings to the Hibernian School. We shall want a Master perhaps, and though I don't promise that you shall be appointed yet I think you had better stand candidate for it; for believe me Mr. Lamb that although I should be ever so much prejudiced in your favour yet if I thought another candidate would fill the place better I would vote against you.

Lamb

I think it right and just that governors of every public institution should act in the same manner.

COLONEL HANDFIELD

Will you stand candidate?

LAMB

I would rather remain in the situation I am in. I shall write again to general Calvert. I hope through his interest I may at least receive his Majesty's bounty as an out pensioner.

COLONEL HANDFIELD

General Calvert can do a great deal for you, he is at the fountain head.

LAMB

I intend to write. Good morning to you gentlemen.

GENL. CLINTON & COL. HANDFIELD.

Good morning to you Mr. Lamb, we shan't forget you.

I was forgotten by these gentlemen. And I thank God that I was forgotten. Indeed many places which are at the disposal of great men are very unfavourable to piety and the self denying religion of the blessed Jesus. Perhaps my heavenly Father foresaw that if I had gotten the situation I desired, I would be greatly exposed to many snares and troubles which I would not in all probability have been able to bear.

"Seekest thou great things for thy self" (said the prophet to Baruch) "Seek them not." I am sure that a good conscience is a continual feast and enough for a happy life. This I can enjoy in the situation I have filled for near forty years past.

I now confined my views to the pension, in order to this I sent genl. Calvert the following letter in which I enclosed my Memorial to the Duke of York.

> Dublin January 7th 1809
>
> Honoured Sir
>
> I feel most sensibly the weight of the obligations under which you & Colonel Mackenzie have placed me, owing to your extreme kindness in recommending me to the Quarter

Master general of Ireland, the general declared it would be very grateful to his mind in serving me, but it did not occur to him in what manner it could be done. Colonel Handfield to whom he introduced me upon hearing my name said "I think I know that name very well, did you not make your escape into New York from general Burgoyne's army." I said I was taken prisoner twice in America and had made my escape—he said I remember you very well. He asked me what was my object in writing to you—I said that as I was in the decline of life, and had a large family to maintain I humbly hoped that through your interest I might obtain his Majesty's bounty as an out pensioner, he said that it was in the power of general Calvert to do a great deal for me and hinted that it would be best for me again to apply to you upon this subject.

I feel a very great reluctance of giving you so much trouble knowing how much your attention is occupied by other important duties however I am led to hope, that the state of an old soldier who had often the honour of obeying your command and of fighting by your side, will not fail to attract your regard in some degree. I therefore venture to send for your perusal, the enclosed memorial to his Royal Highness the Duke of York, which if it would not be too presuming to ask so great a favour, you would be pleased to present to his Royal Highness convinced that your interest, and recommendation would procure for me that favour which would make my declining years comfortable.

I am
&c &c
R. Lamb

He was discharged without the pension usually given for past services, and being frequently advised by his friends to apply for it, in 1809, (twenty-five years after receiving his discharge) he memorialed His Royal Highness the Duke of York, and was graciously favoured by an immediate compliance with the Prayer of his Petition. He submits the Memorial and its Answer, in gratitude to the illustrious individual, who so promptly condescended to notice it as he did.

Dublin, January 7, 1809.

To his Royal Highness the Duke of York, Commander in Chief of his Majesty's forces; the memorial of R. Lamb, late Serjeant in the Royal Welch Fuzileers,

Humbly Sheweth,

That Memorialist served in the Army twelve years, in the 9th and 23d Regiments of Foot, eight years of which was in America; under the command of Generals Burgoyne and Cornwallis; during which time, he was in Six pitched Battles, Four Sieges, several important Expeditions, was twice taken prisoner, and as often made his escape to the British Army; viz. First, in 1778, when prisoner with General Burgoyne's Army, he escaped, with two men, whom he brought with him to General Sir Henry Clinton, at New-York; Secondly, in 1782, when taken with Lord Cornwallis's Army, he eluded the vigilance of the American guards, and conducted under his command, seven men to Sir Guy Carleton, the then Commander in Chief in said City, to both of whom he gave most important Intelligence respecting the enemy's Army, for which Service he was appointed by General Birch, then commandant of the City, his first Clerk, and Adjutant to the Merchants' Corps of Volunteers there.

That in the Battle of Camden, in South Carolina, he had the honor of carrying the Regimental Colours, and immediately after was appointed temporary Surgeon to the Regiment, having had some little knowledge of physic, and received the approbation of all his Officers for his care of the sick and wounded.

That at the battle of Guilford Court-House, in North Carolina; he had the heartfelt pleasure of saving Lord Cornwallis from being taken prisoner, and begs leave with profound deference to state, that he was always chosen one of the first Serjeants to execute any enterprize that required intrepidity, decision and judgment for its accomplishment.

That Memorialist being now far advanced in life, humbly solicits your Royal Highness to recommend him for a military pension, which would smooth his declining years, and be most gratefully received as a remuneration for the many times he has risked his life and limbs in his Majesty's service.

That for the truth of these facts, he most humbly refers to General H. Calvert and Colonel Mackenzie.[8]

To which Memorial the following Answer was received.

Adjutant General's Office

The Adjutant-General informs Serjeant Roger Lamb, that the usual Authority has been given by the Secretary at War, for placing him upon the Out Pension of Chelsea Hospital, dispensing with his personal appearance before the Board.

Horse-Guards, 25*th Jan*. 1809.

Having thus brought this volume to a conclusion, I have only to solicit the indulgence of the candid, and the protection of the loyal reader. My wish has been to state *facts* as I knew they happened, in opposition to that tissue of falsehood, which but too many writers have produced on the subject. To elegance of composition I prefer no claim; but I think, on such matters as the revolution of governments, it is the duty of every man to let the present and the future ages know those *truths* with which he is acquainted, and not to lock them up in his own breast, until the grave closes on all communication, and buries them in oblivion for ever.

If any circumstances have been misrepresented, accident and not intention was the cause. Since the fourth number of this work was

8. Copies of Lamb's letter to General Calvert and his memorial to the Duke of York, with minor variations in wording and punctuation, are in Royal Hospital, Chelsea: Discharge Documents of Pensioners, WO 121/93/46, TNA.

printed, the Author has been informed, in the account of the battle of Camden, particular mention ought to have been made of the 33d regiment. The services which they rendered on that day, were long the theme of the soldiers and officers present.

Thus, under the assistance of the Almighty, has this account been brought to a period. It has not been unattended by many impedimental circumstances. The heavy duties of a crowded school frequently compelled the Author to break in on the hours of rest, in order to finish the narrative. This produced sickness, an alarming sickness, that at one time seemed to threaten life itself. Providence in mercy spared the Author; but it was to consign a son (a beloved child!) to the grave. Amidst personal and family afflictions, therefore has this journal been finished. Had the Author been more at his ease, it might in some points, perhaps, have been better executed. But it would be superfluous in him again to press on the Reader's attention, that the flowers of literature are not to be expected from an old soldier, whose only object in the publication was the unfolding of truth in defence of his country's honor, and the humanity of her officers. He shall have his reward "if he can be numbered among the writers who gave ardour to virtue, and confidence to truth."

On Friday morning January 27th 1809 my daughter Margaret was employed at the fire preparing the childrens breakfast her bib took fire which communicated itself to her frock and petticoat and in a moment all her cloaths were in a blaze. Hannah was minding the two little girls Alicia and Ann (as their mother was gone out) perceiving her sister Margaret all in a blaze and the flame rapidly ascending, she lay down the child Alicia on the carpet and flew to her assistance at the same time gave a dreadful cry—father, father. At that moment I was dressing myself in the closet and hearing the awful cry of Hannah which pierced my very heart I ran out of the closet and beheld my poor child Margaret standing upright endeavouring with her little hands to keep down the blaze which was rapidly advancing to her head. She never said one word but stood with horror in her countenance, immediately I clasped myself about her and pressed her burning cloaths with my arms and body at the same time endeavouring to keep the flame away from her body. After some time I succeeded. What was very extraordinary she received no damage, and I was but slightly burned.

It was on the 16th of December 1814 my family experienced the protecting care of our heavenly Father. A violent S. W. gale which was perhaps as tempestious as ever occurred in Dublin blew down the stack of chimneys over our bed chamber the fall was so great that three or four rafters were broken the bricks rested upon the roof and appeared like a wall but were permitted to go no further. By this storm all the back part of the counselor Campbells house in York Street fell by which three of this female domesticks were killed. A stack of chimneys in Kearn's Hotel tumbling upon the roof was forced through every floor to the very kitchen. In this storm innumerable accidents happened in all quarters of the city, such as houses unroofed, skylights demolished, scaffolds prostrated and sheds thrown down. The lamp posts leading to the suburbs, were generally blown down. Twenty of the largest trees in the College park were torn up by the roots, and there were very few houses in the City which did not sustain some injury. The oldest mariners said that they never witnessed such a storm.

Signal displays of mercy, kindness and providential care of God, should be particularly remembered. When we recollect, that we deserve nothing at his hands, and that the debt of gratitude is all the debt we can pay, in it we should be cheerful, fervent and frequent. An ungrateful heart is an unfeeling, unloving, unbelieving and disobedient heart.

December 8th 1815 This day the Lord laid his chastening rod upon me. I was attacked with a severe pain in my head, a pain in my stomach and violent cramps. I was near death. But I found the bridge strong enough to pass over. The captive desired liberty and the exile his beloved home. While in my greatest agony my class met and prayers were offered up for me.

February 25, 1817. I am weak by my soul is kept in peace.

Portrait of Roger Lamb late in his life by engravers M. H. & J. W. Allen of Dublin from a life drawing by Dublin artist Nicholas Brennan. Methodist Historical Society of Ireland.

January 23, 1818. My days are spent in innocent pleasure instructing my scholars. And my nights in sweet repose in the arms and under the inspection of my best beloved.

I have lived for others since I was eleven years of age. Have I not paid my due proportion to society: May I not now in the 68th year of my age be honourably dismissed to live for myself.

This is the Copy of my Will

Many are "Smit with the rage canine of dying rich"

All I have to bequeath my children are a few old books, and manuscripts and the image of my life.

Perhaps I may die without having any debts to discharge, but I am certain I will leave no wealth to dispose of.

My prayer now is—

"When soon or late we reach the coast,
Oer life's rough ocean driven;
May we be found—no wanderer lost,

A family in heaven." Roger Lamb—July 10th 1824

I have much comfort in all my children, and some what the more that, by the Divine Providence we not only live in the same City, in the same street but in the same house, and that house where they were born, and the very next door to the house of God where we all attend. Hallelujah! August 29th 1824.

45 years are elapsed since I fought in this battle [Guilford Courthouse]

42 years are elapsed since I landed in Dublin

33 years are elapsed since I was elected Master of the Methodist Free School

Witness my hand and a heart couched with some degree of gratitude.

March 19th, 1826

I am now come to the very evening and sunset of life. I am in the 72d year of my age. O what a blessing to live and die a Christian. May it be said of a truth when I am gone, Earth has lost, and heaven has gained a child of God.

I am now in my centry box in Whitefriar Lane thirty years; my situation is quite suited to my little strenght; I may do as much or as little as I please, according to my weakness; and I have an advantage which I can have no where else in such a degree—my little field of action is just at my bedroom, so that if I happen to overdo myself, I have but to step from my school to my bed and from by bed to my grave in the cabbage garden. I am sweetly helped to drink the dregs of life, and to carry with ease the daily cross. I am not long for this world. I <u>see</u> it, I <u>feel</u> it, and by looking at death and his conqueror, I fight before hand my last battle with that last enemy whom my blessed Lord hath overcome for me.

Much of my life has been passed in a dependant state, and consequently I have received many favours in the opinion of those at whose expence I have been maintained, yet I do not feel in my heart any burning gratitude or tumultuous affection to many of them.

I have written this book chiefly for my children that they may be able, after my discease to have those things always in remembrance. We should oblige our children in many things.

I may well say that my last days are my best. For I now spend my days without cares and my nights without groans.

APPENDIX

Journal of three serjeants of the 23rd Regiment, who made their escape from York, in Pennsylvania, the 1st March, and arrived at New York the 23rd March 1782[1]

A Sentimental Journal of 21 days.

Left our confinement 1st March and received from Captain Saumerez one dollar each, crossed the Susquehanna 2d March paid two dollars to our Guide that conducted us over the ice. 3d March crossed Conastoga Creek & paid one dollar. 4th March changed our cloathing among friends. Read His Majesty's speech to them which we coppy'd from the Pennsylvania Journal, the[y] seem'd rejoiced being afraid of a general evacuation of His Majesty's troops from America. 5th March conducted us 25 Miles to the cross keys 30 miles from Philadelphia expected a friend in the Landlord but happen'd to prove otherwise having discovered ourselves he seem'd excautious & told us our affairs was desperate & that we need not expect any indulgence from him. We reasoned in a Politick manner & enlarged upon the success that would attend his Majesty's Arms the ensuing Campagne, he was often carryed he said with that hopes but seen no prospect in the accomplishment & that our former friends in that state was almost diminished to a Cypher as for his part he had entirely chang'd his principles seeing such a gloomy prospect of success. Finding him so hardened we beged him to direct us to a friend, he would not. We told him if he would do us no

1. Sir Henry Clinton Papers Vol. 191:47, William L. Clements Library.

good we hoped he do us no harm, as there was at that time Continental Officers in the house, he seem'd uneasy at our stay in his house being on the Public road. We set of very much down hearted and kept the road but unfortunately met a party of militia that was returning from conducting a party of prisoners to Philadelphia, examined us & fetch us back to Lancaster & put us in Jail.

11th March made our escape & proceeded through the wood directing our course to the Valley forge, where our worthy friends the Quakers are thickly settled. The[y] received us with the greatest cordiality expressing the greatest veneration & Loyalty to His Majesty and assisted us in our distress and hoped we would mention their attachment & zeal to the Commander in Chief if we arrived safe in N. York. The[y] are grievously oppressed and pay more taxes in one year now than in 21 years before. The[y] conducted us across Schuylkill four miles above Sweads ford and directed us to friends which are numerous between the rivers, in short whole townships are attached to Government. 15th March crossed Delaware four miles above Trenton found our friends greatly diminished in the Jerseys & very difficult to march upon the account of the swamps as we were obliged to steer through the woods, lay in the woods several days for want of a guide, came to Princetown & pass for deserters from Staten Island, found friends in Hopewell township five miles from Princetown, remain'd among them till we could procure a guide to carry us to N. York. We got a man that generally carried prisoners to our lines, but was affraid at that time to come with us, as Captain Hyler was in Brunswick & kept a guard on the bridge as a Gunboat was building there. However we gave him what money we had which had a great affect upon him. 17th March at night came to a town & losed our guide. Our affairs being desperate we resolv'd to guide ourselves, came to a house and obliged the man to put us on the right road or death should be his portion, however he happened to be a friend and was surprised he said at our boldness but knew the British was always intrepid in any dangerous enterprize.

18th March directed us to a friend which conducted us & avoided Brunswick

19th March left destitute of friends we proceeded to South Amboy rambl'd along shore all night but could not find a craft.

20th Concealed ourselves in the woods 3 miles from S. Amboy up Brunswick river, seen Captain Skinners Galley in the river. 21st Hunger making us desperate came to a house on the shore side and discovered our intention, proved to be good friends & put us aboard the galley, beg'd us to mention their names at Head Quarters. We told them their was numbers more on the road if the[y] would assert them the[y] might be assured of a bounty from the Commander in Chief.

Johnson, Calver—the mens Names that fetch'd us to the galley lives 3 miles from S. Amboy up Brunswick River

Our Total expence—£9.15.9

R. Lamb

Sergt. R. W. Fuzileers

SOURCES

This book is composed of writings by Roger Lamb from the following sources:

An Original and Authentic Journal of Occurrences during the late American War, from its commencement to the year 1783 (Dublin: Wilkinson & Courtney, 1809), pages 66-71, 104-105, 107-112, 135, 137-144, 158-160, 163-166, 193-196, 208-209, 252-263, 268-273, 293-295, 302-306, 341-355, 358-359, 361-363, 388-415, 434-438

Memoir of his Own Life (Dublin: J. Jones, 1811), pages 5-8, 34-35, 37, 47-48, 61-62, 64, 66-68, 71-75, 89-91, 94-96, 102-104, 106-110, 113-114, 117, 138-139, 160-161, 164-165, 167-168, 172-175, 177-179, 181-183, 189-194, 199-200, 202-203, 212, 222, 232, 234-235, 242-245, 247, 250-253, 264-265, 270-271, 282, 289-292.

Journal of three serjeants of the 23rd Regiment, who made their escape from York, in Pennsylvania, the 1st March, and arrived at New York the 23rd March 1782. William L. Clements Library: Sir Henry Clinton Papers Vol. 191 fol. 47.

Roger Lamb's Commonplace Book. Methodist Historical Society of Ireland Archive, Belfast, pages 28, 34, 43, 46, 48, 53, 56-57, 59, 72, 74, 82, 108-130, 134-137, 139, 142-147, 150-151, 157, 171, 191, 206-208, 214-215, 222-223, 226

FURTHER READING

On Roger Lamb's later life:

Kenneth Ferguson, "Roger Lamb: Soldier and Writer, Schoolmaster at Whitefriar Street," *Bulletin of the Methodist Historical Society of Ireland* Vol. 23 No. 2 (2018), 107-190.

J. O. Bonsall, "Memoir of Mr. Roger Lamb, of Dublin," *Wesleyan-Methodist Magazine* 3rd Series Vol 10 (November 1831),729-734

On Roger Lamb's commonplace book:

Don N. Hagist, "Unpublished Military Writings of Roger Lamb, Soldier in the 1775–1783 American War, Part 1." *Journal of the Society for Army Historical Research* 89, no. 360 (Winter 2011): 280-290; "Unpublished Military Writings of Roger Lamb, Soldier in the 1775–1783 American War, Part 2." *Journal of the Society for Army Historical Research* 90, no. 362 (Summer 2012): 77-89.

On British Soldiers during the American Revolution:

Don N. Hagist, *Noble Volunteers: the British Soldiers who fought the American Revolution* (Yardley, PA: Westholme, 2020)

Don N. Hagist, *British Soldiers, American War: Voices of the American Revolution* (Yardley, PA: Westholme, 2012)

Thomas Sullivan, *From Redcoat to Rebel: The Thomas Sullivan Journal*, ed. Joseph Lee Boyle (Bowie, MD: Heritage Books, 1997)

On the 1777 and 1781 campaigns:

Don Troiani and Eric Schnitzer, *Don Troiani's Campaign to Saratoga—1777* (Mechanicsburg, PA: Stackpole Books, 2019)

Carl P. Borick, *A Gallant Defense: The Siege of Charleston, 1780* (Columbia: University of South Carolina Press, 2003)

Andrew Waters, *To the End of the World: Nathanael Greene, Charles Cornwallis, and the Race to the Dan* (Yardley, PA: Westholme, 2020)

John R. Maass, *The Road to Yorktown: Jefferson, Lafayette and the British Invasion of Virginia* (Mount Pleasant, SC: Arcadia Publishing, 2015)

INDEX

Acland, John Dyke, 60
Acteus transport, 93
agents, 24
Albany, 46, 60
Allamance Creek, 105-106
Allen, J. W., 171
Allen, M. H., 171
Amboy, 140-141, 143
Andre, John, 83
Anticosti, 29
Arbuthnot, Mariot, 90, 93
Arnold, Benedict, 31, 35-36, 61
Ashley River, 90, 92

Balfour, Nesbit, 19, 84, 115, 146, 149, 160-161
Baron de Kalb, 96
batteaux, 33, 35, 37, 40, 51, 53, 63
Bay of St. Paul, 30
bayonet, 8, 13, 21, 45, 57, 63, 89, 91, 95-96, 102-103, 107, 109, 126
Beattie's Ford, 101, 104
Belfast, xii, 14
Belsham, William, 86-89, 139-140
Bemis Heights, 61
Bennington, 40, 51
Birch, Samuel, 145, 160, 167
black-hole, 12, 22
Blue Hills, 67
bombardier, 101
Boone, Daniel, 122
Boyd's Ferry, 105
Brennan, Nicholas, 171
Breymann, Heinrich Christoph, 56, 61
Brigade of Guards, 87, 101, 103, 107-110, 113
British Legion, 93, 95
Brooks, William, 27-28, 73-74
Brunswick, 31, 139
Buchanan, James, 28, 72-73
Bunker's-hill, 68
Burgess, William P., 155
Burgoyne, John, xiv, 14, 33, 36-37, 40-41, 46, 48, 50, 52, 56, 59-62, 64, 72, 82, 84, 97, 100, 118, 127-130, 141, 145, 158-159, 163, 166-167
Buy, Johann Christian du, 110

Calvert, Harry, 84-85, 150-151, 158, 162, 164-166, 168
Camden, 94, 96, 98, 116, 159, 167, 169
Camille frigate, 87
Canada, xi, 11, 27, 30-31, 33-35, 37-40, 42, 53, 72
cannons, 32, 34-35, 37, 43, 57-58, 60, 62, 64, 93, 96, 108-109
Cape Breton, 29
Cape de Retz, 29
Cape Fear River, 116

Cape Rosieres, 29
Cape Torment, 30
carcasses, 93
card-playing, 15
Carleton, Guy, 31, 35-36, 72, 164, 167
Castletown, 44
Catawba River, 103-104
Caudres, 29
Cavan, 5
Chamblee, 34, 37
Champagne, Forbes, 97, 159
Chapelizod, 36
Charlestown, 19, 86, 90, 92-93, 98, 115, 146, 159-160
Charlotte Ville, 98, 131
Chelsea Hospital, 168
Cheraw-Hill, 99
Clarke, Sampson, 22-23
Clerke, Francis-Carr, 61
Clinton, Henry, 83-84, 86, 90, 93-94, 131, 145, 159, 162-165, 167
Clinton, William Henry, 162
Club-law, 6
Collier, George, 87
Collins, Charles, 132
colours, 94, 96, 159, 167
Connor, Richard, 129
Continental Congress, x, 31, 34, 67-68, 128
Convention Army, 129
Coote, Eyre, 127
Cork, xi, 17, 23-26
Cornwallis, Charles, xv, 18, 48, 86, 94, 96, 98-101, 104-106, 111, 114-119, 128-129, 157, 159, 161, 163, 167
Count de Grasse, 118
Count Rochambeau, 117
court-martial, 10, 22-23, 76
Cowpens, 98-99
Cross Creek, 115-116
Crown Point, 31, 34-36, 40, 42
Crumer, Jane, 156
Cunningham, Thomas, 21-22

Dan River, 100, 105
Davidson, William Lee, 101
Deep River, 106, 116
Delaware River, 138
desertion, 7, 12, 76, 84, 130, 137, 141
Detroit, 11, 38
Devaco, 54
Douglas, James, 45
Dovecote, 54
Downpatrick, 14, 24
drill, see training
Drogheda road, 25
Dublin, ix-x, xv, 1-6, 11, 13-14, 17-18, 22-25, 36, 49, 53, 142, 149, 152-156, 158, 161-162, 164-165, 167, 170-172
Duke of York, 152, 165-168

Earl of Moira, 7, 14, 96-97
8th Regiment of Foot, 11, 26, 38
18th Regiment of Foot, 5
80th Regiment of Foot, 127
11th Massachusetts Regiment, 43
exercise, see training

Fairfield, 88
Field officers, 58
field pieces, see cannons
53rd Regiment of Foot, 26, 37
firelock, see musket
flogging, 7, 10, 12
Forbes, Gordon, 55
Fort Ann, 40, 46-47, 49-50, 69
Fort Chartres, 5
Fort Edward, 40, 50-52
Fort Henry, 52
Fort Miller, 40, 52
Fort Moultrie, 93
Francis, Ebenezer, 43-45
Frazer, Simon, 32, 37, 43-44, 60-61
Frederick-town, 120, 122, 124-125
Freeman's Farm, 57

galley, 36, 43, 87
Gallows-green, 20
Garth, George, 87
Gartside, Abraham, 84
Gates, Horatio, 64, 94-95, 97-98, 159
gauntlet, 47, 67, 70-71
George III, 139
German troops, 31, 38, 40-41, 44, 51, 56, 60-61, 69, 76, 84, 90, 139
Gloucester Point, 118, 120, 146

gondolas, 36
Gordon, James, 127
Grant, Robert, 44
Greene, Nathanael, 98-99, 104-106, 115-116
Greenfield, 88
Gregory, Isaac, 96
grenadiers, 37, 43-44, 51, 55-56, 60, 107-108
Guernsey, 130
Guildford Court-House, 105-106, 108-109, 113-114, 116, 157, 159
Gunn, William, 84, 141

Haggart, James, 45
halberts, 12
Halifax, 87
Hall, Francis, 103
Hamilton, James, 37
Hamilton's Ford, 99
Handfield, Charles, 84, 163-166
Haw, 105-106
Hesse-Hanau, 31
Hesse-Kassel, 31
Hessians, 31, 111
Hibbertown, 43
Hibernian School, 162
Hill, John, 46-47
Hillsborough, 105
Holy Thursday, 39
Horse-Guards, 168
Howard, Francis, 5
Howard, John Eager, 99
Howard, William, 1, 5-6
Howe, William, xi, 17-18, 139
Hubbardton, 43
Hudson River, 40, 52-54, 63, 67, 75, 82
Huger, Isaac, 104
Huntington Bay, 88
Hussar galley, 87

Indian file, 18, 48, 132
Inflexible, 35, 41
Irwine's Ferry, 105

James's Island, 90-93
Johnson, John, 38

Kearn's Hotel, 170
Killishandra, 5
Kilmainham, 164
King's Bridge, 79, 81-82, 146, 160
Knyphausen, Wilhelm von, 90

La fete Dieu, 39
Lake Champlain, xiii, 31, 34, 40-41
Lake George, 43, 52-53
Lake Ontario, 12
Lamb, Margaret, 169
Latouche, John David, 163
Lee, Charles, 136
Lee, Henry, 105-106, 136
Leslie, Alexander, 94, 104, 106, 108-111
light infantry, 17-18, 37, 43, 44, 55, 56, 60, 95, 99, 107, 108
Ligonier, Edward, 17
Lincoln, Benjamin, 93-94
Lindsay, Alexander (Lord Balcarras), 44-45, 61
Little York, 128-129, 146
Long Island, 88, 127, 160
Lord Ligonier, 17
Lord Rawdon, 14, 95, 97
Loyalists, x, 14, 72, 93, 97, 105, 132, 142-144

Mackenzie, Frederick, 145, 162, 164-165, 168
Maitland, Augustus, 110
Bolton, Mason, 7, 11-12, 14, 20, 26
manual exercise, see training
Maria, 35
McGuire, Patrick, 65
McLeod, John, 106
M'Cowan's Ford, 101
Merchants Corps of volunteers, 146, 160, 167
Methodist Free School, 162, 172
Methodist Historical Society of Ireland, 23, 47, 69, 71, 103, 113, 125, 137, 143, 171
Methodist Society, 152, 164
militias, 53, 64, 67, 93-94, 96, 99, 104, 106, 109, 118, 130, 146
Milton, John, 112
Money, John, 48-49
Monk's Corner, 93
Montgomery, William, 24, 37, 49

Montreal, 12, 37, 72
Morgan, Daniel, 99, 104
Mount Independence, 42
muskets, 8, 13, 18, 44, 45-46, 103, 111
muster rolls, 9, 23, 26, 28, 65, 84-85, 132, 141

Nesbit, William, 33, 37
Newfoundland, 28-29
Newgate Jail, 20
New Haven, 87-89
New Jersey Volunteers, 144
New London, 88
New York City Militia, 146
New York harbor, 148
Niagara, 11, 38
Ninety-Six, 19, 99
9th Regiment of Foot, xiii, 7-9, 11, 13-14, 16-17, 20, 23, 26, 28, 37, 46-49, 55, 59, 65, 69, 72, 84, 119, 128-129, 141, 145, 158, 167
North Carolina militia, 96, 106
North Edisto, 90
North River, 77, 79-80, 86
North Wall, 2
Norton, Chapel, 107, 111
Norwark, 88
Notre Dame, 29

The Odyssey of Homer, 147
O'Hara, Charles, 104, 107-109
Ontario, 12
out-pension examining board, 148, 150, 153, 161, 168

Paps of Montani, 29
parallels, 92-93
Parks, Thomas, 151
Parliament, 164
Paterson, James, 90
Pedee River, 99
Phillips, William, 37, 56
picquets, 55, 58
Pope, Alexander, 147
Porterfield, Charles, 95
Portsmouth, 148
Powell, Henry Watson, 37
Pringle, Thomas, 35
Prospect-hill, 67-69

Quakers, 53-54, 106, 115, 134
Quarter Guards, 61
Quebec, xi, 17, 24, 26, 30-32, 37-38, 52

radeau, 35
Ramsay, David, 86, 88-89, 140
Ramsey's Mill, 116
Rawdon, George, 7, 14, 95, 97, 116
redoubts, 34, 117
Reedy Fork, 105-106, 115
regimentals, see uniforms
Regiment of Bose, 106, 109-111, 116
Richmond, 100
River du China, 38
Royal Artillery, 36-37, 57, 99, 106, 109
Royal George, 41
Royal Highlanders, 38
Royal Highness, 166-168
Royal Hospital, 164
Royal Irish Artillery, 36
Royal Navy, 35, 144
Royal Square barracks, 22
Royal Welch Fusiliers, see 23rd Regiment of Foot
Rugeley's Mills, 94
Ruggles, Timothy, 72
Rutland, 68, 71-72, 128

Saintfield, 7, 14, 16
Salisbury, 17
Sandy Hook, 90, 148
Santie Ferry, 92
saps, 94
Saratoga, xiv, 14, 40, 51, 54, 57, 61-63, 65, 67, 84, 97, 119, 131, 158
Saumarez, Thomas, 130
Savannah, 90
Schnitzer, Eric, 13, 59, 91
Schuyler, Philip, 50, 63
Scorpion sloop, 87
71st Regiment of Foot, 95, 106, 109, 122-123
Shelly, Henry, 26, 49
Shrimpton, John, 45
Simpson's Port, 92
64th Regiment of Foot, 94
62nd Regiment of Foot, 26, 38, 45, 56
Skeensborough, 43, 46, 49-50
Skinner, Cortland, 144

Skinner, John McGregor, 144
small pox, 34
Society of Friends, 53
Sorel, 31-33
Specht, Johann Friedrich, 38
Spooner, Bathsheba, 28, 72-73
Spooner, Joshua, 28, 72-73
spying, 47, 83
squad, 19
Staten Island, 140, 142, 144
Stedman, Charles, 107
Stewart, James, 108
Still Water, 54
stirabout, 133
St. John's, 34
St. Lawrence River, 28-29, 32-33
Stranger Friend Society, 164
subalterns, 58
Sugar Hill, 42
Sullivan's Island, 93
Susquehannah River, 130, 146
sutlers, 41
Swettenham, George, 16

taprooms, 21
Tarleton, Banastre, 93, 96, 99, 104, 106-107, 111
Tarrant's Tavern, 104
Taylor, William, 20
3rd Regiment of Foot Guards, 61
31st Regiment of Foot, 26
34th Regiment of Foot, 26, 38, 45
37th Regiment of Foot, 127
33rd Regiment of Foot, 18-19, 107-108, 116, 127-128, 169
Three Rivers, 31-32, 38
Ticonderoga, 36-37, 42, 46, 51-53
Towns Arch, 22
Trading Ford, 104
Training, 8-9, 12, 17-20, 38, 45-46
Trinity Point, 29
Troublesome Creek, 105, 115
Tryon, William, 87-88
20th Regiment of Foot, 26, 37, 56-58, 60
21st Regiment of Foot, 26, 37, 56
24th Regiment of Foot, 26, 32, 37, 44-45, 55-56, 60
29th Regiment of Foot, 26, 45
23rd Regiment of Foot, Royal Welch Fusiliers, x, xiii, 18-19, 84-85, 91, 95, 97, 101, 112, 117, 122, 130, 132, 141, 145, 151, 158-159, 167
Tybee, 90

uniforms, xii, 13, 15, 23, 59, 91, 103, 124

Valcour Island, 35
Valley Forge, 136
Van Brigade, 37
vanguard, 33, 63
Volunteers of Ireland, 95, 97
von Riedesel, Friedrich, 38, 41, 44, 57, 60, 62

wadding, 58
Wando River, 92
Wappo, 90, 92
War Office, 16, 24, 148, 158
Washington, George, 86, 98, 118, 140, 160
Washington, William, 98-99, 109
Waterbury, David, 36
Waterford, 7, 9-10, 14
Webster, James, 18, 95, 97-98, 101, 104, 106-109, 112, 116
Wedzell's Mill, 106
Wesley, John, 4, 155-156
Westmeath, 5
Westropp, Richard, 49
Whitefriar Lane, 172
Williams, Griffith, 57, 61
Williams, Otho Holland, 104
Wilmington, 115-116
Winchester, 119-120, 128, 148, 161
Wives of soldiers, 11, 16, 28, 49-50, 53-54, 72, 129

Yadkin River, 104
York, 118
Yorktown, 117, 119-120, 123, 128, 131, 159
Young, Ann, 156